MIDDLE SPACE
YOUTH WORK

MIDDLE SPACE YOUTH WORK

Loyd Harp

MONARCH
BOOKS

Published by **Monarch Books**
www.lionhudson.com

Part of the SPCK Group

SPCK, 36 Causton Street, London, SW1P 4ST

ISBN 978 1 80030 012 5
e-ISBN 978 1 80030 053 8

First edition 2022

Acknowledgments
Scripture quotations taken from The Holy Bible, New International Version® NIV®
Copyright © 1973 1978 1984 2011 by Biblica, Inc. TM
Used by permission. All rights reserved worldwide.

A catalogue record for this book is available from the British Library

Printed and bound in the UK, January 2022, LH26

Contents

Introduction

Like many of you, I got into youth ministry out of a desire to share the love of God with young people. I grew up in a medium-sized suburban church in central Oklahoma. This part of the United States is a very blue-collar (working-class) area with a strong affinity for country music and do-it-yourself projects. Our church had a strong youth group with great leaders, both salaried and volunteer. Like most teenagers I felt out of place in the world, never feeling like I fit in anywhere. This was intensified by my situation at home. My father had left me and my mother when I was less than a year old, and though mom remarried, my new adopted dad and I never had much in common. I didn't realize it at the time, but Lakeside Church had taken on the role of a father in my life. Having missed out on growing up with my real father, and not having a close relationship to the man I called "dad", it was no wonder I struggled to fit in anywhere.

But church... the church, and specifically the youth group... that was where life made sense! It was *my* space. It was where I fit. It was where I received validation from both male and female role models. It was where – over time – I was able to eventually call God my Father, something I struggled with cognitively when I was younger. It was also where my call to full-time ministry was recognized and affirmed. I was fifteen when I first heard that call. It's hard to describe what happened that night. My mother and I had gone to my aunt's church in another town to perform some music ministry. While we were preparing that evening, I had a deep feeling – an innate sense that God was calling me to full-time Christian service. There was no burning bush, just a deep *knowing*.

In many ways it's significant that God called me in an unconventional way. In the area where I grew up, a call to ministry generally meant preaching. The only room for divergence seemed to be whether you'd end up as a full-time pastor or as a travelling evangelist. For my part, I knew God was calling me to full-time ministry, but not necessarily to the traditional clergy. To be honest, I wasn't sure what God was calling me to do. All I knew was that I wanted to serve him and to serve people. I sort of "fell into" youth ministry out of my love for music, the arts, and popular culture. Youth work just seemed a natural extension of who I was.

Many of us have been doing youth ministry for years. A few have been in this for a decade or more. Some of us are just starting out. Yet others who are reading this book are not directly in youth work at all, but are instead church leaders, lay ministers, or even parents. I'm really encouraged by the thought that there's room for all of us at the Round Table of discussion in regards to youth ministry. My hope is that it does not matter which of those categories best describes you; we can all find some space in this book to gather around a strategic approach to working with young people.

A few years ago, I was having a bit of a dry spell, both spiritually and in my youth work. I was tired. At this point in my journey I had been working on the front lines of youth work for roughly fifteen years in different settings. Now in my forties, I was probably feeling my age a bit too. While on a weekend youth camp (Soul Survivor, for those who know it), I met with God. Or rather, he met with me. I was having one of those moments that most of us have had at some point. I found myself asking, "Lord, do you want me to keep doing this, or should I be looking for something else?" In my little prayer space at the back of that massive, sweaty, crowded, noisy outdoor marquee, I began thinking about all the youth camps I'd gone to when I was a youngster.

I was thinking about all the times and ways God had met with me at camps in Henrietta and Tishomingo, Oklahoma. I was remembering all the youth retreats, overnight camping trips, the friends I'd made, and my call to ministry as a teen. God was showing me something through those memories and those experiences. They had been the most significant moments and formative experiences of my life. Then it dawned on me. That is why I'm in youth ministry. I loved my youth group and those transformative experiences so much that I had – without realizing it – devoted my whole life to recreating that ethos for others. It was a eureka moment for me. I remember thinking, "Lord, if this is what you want me to do for the rest of my life, I am OK with that."

Nothing can take away the significance of impacting a young person's life in a positive way. Perhaps you can relate to my story in some way. Ultimately, you probably do Christian youth work because you want young people to encounter Christ. Or because you want to shape their lives in a positive direction. Or because you want to reach out to those who haven't had that positive and life-changing experience of being involved in a Christian youth group.

So why this book? At the very minimum, what I hope to accomplish is to give you a tool for reflection. So often in youth ministry, we are doers. We like to get on with things, and nobody had better slow us down! Shoot first, and ask questions later. The downside is that we don't often take time to thoughtfully consider what it is that we actually do, nor why we do it. Why? Because, as doers, we are often so caught up in action. We know what youth ministry is. We do the small group Bible studies, and the pizza parties, and the bowling outings, the paintball tournaments, the camps, and... you get the picture. But in all of those wonderful things, what are we actually trying to accomplish? Why are we doing them? Have you ever stopped to ask: what is the goal of our youth ministry? Together we are going to ask ourselves these questions and a few more, looking at not only the *what* of youth ministry, but also the *why* and the *how*. By the time you are reading this book, we will also have gone through the Covid-19 pandemic, which has forced yet another cultural shift, imploring us to explore the ins and outs of contemporary youth ministry and what it all means.

After taking some time to reflect on our own youth ministry practices and stated goals, we're going to look at some existing models of youth work. Some things we'll affirm, and others we will critique where needed. We'll spend a little more time looking at Attractional youth work models, which are particularly common in the United States, but also have some holds in the United Kingdom and elsewhere, largely due to the American influence. This model is especially prominent in larger churches – often called megachurches when attendance of the church reaches 1,000 people or more in weekend gatherings. However, so often smaller churches try to emulate larger churches and their tools for growth, so Attractional ministry is everywhere.

Finally, the bulk of the book will be dedicated to proposing a new model: "Middle Space" youth work. Middle Space is a simple concept, but one that is fairly revolutionary when it comes to youth ministry. Most youth ministry (and many other church programmes too, including outreach events) takes place within the church walls – that is, within sacred spaces. For our purposes here, we'll call this *our space*. A smaller percentage of innovative youth work (and evangelism) takes place *out there*, or outside the church walls. We'll call this *their space*. Middle

Space proposes a third way: ministry that takes place in space that is neither ours nor theirs, but somewhere in the middle, in a shared space or neutral ground. Although this is sometimes referred to as "third spaces", I have deliberately chosen not to use that term. Middle Space has implications for the type of physical space in which we do ministry, but the implications are much further-reaching than that. Unsurprisingly, it is possible to simply change the location of what we do in ministry (using a third space, for instance), but still use the space in the same way, not changing anything we do, or our approach to the people we want to reach.

The time is right – both culturally and theologically – for us to think about new ways of doing youth work. This is not primarily going to be a book about statistics, or the horrific numbers of young people (and young adults) leaving the church. The numbers are there for those who wish to find them, and we'll consider some of them briefly in order to make the point: big changes are needed in how we do youth ministry. Middle Space youth work is influenced in theology and mission by the Missional Church movement, as well as pioneering approaches to youth work, like Detached youth work and Symbiotic youth work (more on that later). Yet, when all is taken into account, Middle Space emerges as a new model altogether distinct from other approaches.

The Middle Space approach is significant for a number of reasons. First, it is simple. It is not difficult to understand, nor is it difficult to establish. When we began introducing the model in our youth work in rural southern England, it evolved so naturally and organically that I expected everyone to be doing it. The more I looked into youth ministry across the UK and the United States (with my humble apologies to those in other cultural contexts), the more I discovered it is not that widespread, although it does seem to be gaining traction where faith communities value young people both inside and outside the church walls.

Second, Middle Space is significant because it attempts to lower the threshold or barrier between the church and the general culture. We'll talk a little about cultural and theological bridge-building, and the need to create healthy and positive ways to talk about faith in our increasingly secularized world. We'll also examine some of the theology and cultural relevance of so-called sacred spaces and what that means for youth work.

Third, Middle Space rejects outright the unspoken, but all too common notion that Christian youth work must choose between evangelism and discipleship. In fact, a biblical definition of discipleship necessarily involves Good News sharing (evangelism) and further discipleship of those who already know and love the Lord, but who want to go deeper in their relationship with Christ.

Don't worry, it's not all theoretical. We'll also spend lots of time discussing practical issues of youth ministry as it relates to Middle Space: creatively using spaces, renovating buildings, utilizing adult helpers and volunteers, integrating discipleship and evangelism into a singular youth ministry, and ways to capitalize on cross-pollination and bridge-building opportunities. Buckle up, it's going to be an interesting ride!

Reflection Section

Youth workers: Why do you do youth work?

Clergy/church leaders/lay ministers: Why do you care about youth work?

Parents/laypeople: What do you want out of youth work for your children and teens, or those in your church/community?

1

The Essence of Youth Ministry

The first thing we need to do in any book about youth ministry is to think about what youth ministry actually is. Sure, you and I *know* what it is, but how often have we truly reflected on what we do in youth ministry? Youth work and children's work are undertaken by a variety of different people in different settings. Some of us are fortunate enough to get paid to work with young people. Invariably we also rely on a lot of volunteers to assist or, in many cases, lead the work. All of us are in need of some critical reflection on what we do. We hinted at this in the Introduction, and here we want to go a little bit deeper into what we actually do as youth workers.

To help us understand the need of such reflection, I relay here an anecdotal, but absolutely true story. A volunteer children's worker I used to work with and I were once having a conversation about our Sunday groups. Although I worked with the teenagers, there was obviously some overlap with the children's work, so we were discussing how to work together. As we were discussing the groups, and in particular the timings of the morning sessions, she admitted, "Let's be honest – what we're really doing is babysitting them for half an hour."

I was shocked. Although her honesty was refreshing, her blurted-out thoughts held a key to understanding how children's work was being approached in that particular setting. My mind went back to the children's work model I grew up with in Oklahoma. Our volunteer children's pastor was lovingly referred to as "Aunt Clara". Even though we technically shared no blood relationship, there was a deep familial bond because of the way she cared for the children in the group. Week in, week out, she taught us from the Bible, organized the puppet ministry, recruited volunteers to assist – and all unpaid! I have a vivid memory of something she said once, during her teaching, as she was trying to explain God's empathic love for us through Christ. With tears in her eyes and compassion in her voice, she exclaimed, "All I know is that when Jake hurts, Jesus hurts. When Jake is happy, Jesus is happy!" I don't know if Jake still remembers that moment, but I certainly do. To this day, I can't repeat this scene without getting goosebumps! I don't know how much Aunt Clara had reflected on her model of children's ministry, but she certainly had not received any formal training. Nevertheless, I can say with absolute clarity that she did not see what she was doing as simply babysitting, nor merely entertaining children while the adults were having "big church", or worse, "real church". I often use Aunt Clara's story to inspire my volunteers and other youth and children's workers to believe in the power of what they are doing. What are we doing and saying today that children will remember twenty, thirty, or in my case forty years later?

I suspect that the children's worker in my first example wasn't truly primarily concerned with babysitting children for half an hour, but was rather expressing frustrations with the time limitations in that local setting. However, the story does get us thinking about our approach to youth work. Let's take a brief look at a few different models of youth ministry. Although it may be tempting for some youth work veterans to skip over the next few pages ("Why is this guy telling me about youth work models I already know about?"), I recommend that you don't. We're going to be using them to build the case for our new model, as we consider the strengths, weaknesses, contributions, and shortcomings of each of them.

What Do We Do? A Few Dominant Youth Ministry Models

Entertainment/Babysitting

Although there is no formal model called "Babysitting" being taught in colleges, and almost no one would admit this is what they are doing (except for maybe my refreshingly honest friend above), it is indeed a working model in actual practice. People using this model will not generally have thought much about what they are trying to accomplish. They won't have considered questions like, "Are we primarily concerned with evangelism or discipleship, or both?" They don't worry themselves with things like a five-year plan, how to engage the entire family, or how to reach out into the community. Primary concerns in this mode include,

"How much time do we have to fill?" Or similarly, "How can I keep them busy for _____ amount of time?" Or, more subtly, "What activities can I plan for them?" The final question is not a bad one, but if it characterizes the totality of your work with children and young people, it might be time to dig deeper.

As negative as it may seem, there are some useful things to take away from the entertainment model. All of us will use entertainment at some point in our youth ministry. After all, who hasn't hosted a late-night movie marathon: The Lord of the Rings or the Star Wars series, no doubt. If you haven't started one of your sessions with an ice-breaker game, I sincerely doubt you're actually doing youth ministry! Most of us at some point have been plagued with the following scenario: "I have ten minutes to spare. What are we going to do to fill that time?" If you can answer that without a panic, you are benefitting from the positive aspects of entertainment. In fact, the simplest definition of the word entertain is "to hold the attention".[1] Nonetheless, a youth ministry that is built primarily around babysitting or entertainment will not offer much in terms of long-term positive effects on the lives of young people.

Safe Space/Refuge, and Other Specialized Youth Ministries

This youth ministry model is a specialized one that is particularly beneficial in areas where there are intense societal needs or problems. They are often found in areas of urban or rural poverty, areas with high rates of violence, drug and alcohol abuse, or other related issues. As the name implies, proponents of this model seek to create a safe space or refuge for young people from vulnerable or dangerous situations, and it has been utilized by organizations such as Teen Challenge (a drugs and alcohol rehabilitation ministry for young people), or programmes and ministries like the YMCA, Boys and Girls Clubs of America, and the Salvation Army. Although all of us hope that our work with youth does indeed provide a safe space – a refuge from the world at large – it is not our predominant model of youth ministry. The model itself specifically focuses on providing intervention in and/or a shelter from intense life situations.

In addition to the Safe Space or Refuge model, there are other specialized youth ministry models that may have a particular focus.

For instance, a church with a strong music ministry might have a youth choir, band, or orchestra that serves as a youth group in and of itself. Youth drama, dance, and sports teams can function in largely the same way, as well as other mentoring programmes which may involve some combination of Christian discipleship/teaching, paired with a particular emphasis or life skill (technology, the arts, sports, etc.). Often, specialized groups are not run by one local church, but rather by a cooperation of nearby churches, or even a parachurch organization. These organizations do some amazing work, but we want to spend most of our time in this chapter thinking about more common forms of congregational-based youth ministries. In chapter 11, when we look at specific examples of Middle Space ministry, we will consider some innovative approaches involving specialized work with young people.

Standard Church-based Youth Group

One of the most common forms of youth ministry (at least in the United States and the United Kingdom), by my observation, is simply the church youth group. The shape and size of these groups vary greatly, as does the theology, which is generally in keeping with the parent church. Nonetheless, there are a number of elements that are commonly present in such groups:

- *Regular meetings.* Almost all church youth groups will have at least one meeting per week (some will have two or more) that mirror and/or provide an alternative setting to the larger congregation. These meetings take many forms including youth-oriented worship services, Sunday school classes, youth group meetings, small group Bible studies, and so forth. These sessions generally take place in a room within the church building or an adjacent building on the same property. We'll talk more about the use of space a little later, as it is an important, defining theme in Christian youth work.
- *Camps and retreats.* Most church youth groups will create time and space to get away together. These events are strategically planned to create environments of liminality, or spaces where change can occur. As Kenda Creasy Dean puts it, "In youth ministry, liminal practices leverage dissonance for the sake of divine transformation. Thrust into spaces where none of our usual cultural tools work, we are forced to

step back and scan for new ones. In so doing, we observe ourselves and our new situations anew, rethinking our former understandings of God, self, and others."[2] In other words, youth ministries often utilize camps, retreats, and overnight residentials as environments for change. Getting away from the distractions of home, social media, normal peer groups, even the home church helps to create a sense of focus. We'll speak more about the importance of liminal events in chapter 3, but for now it's enough to acknowledge they comprise a key aspect of most forms of church youth ministry.

- *Social events.* What would a youth group be without social events? Pool parties, gaming nights, overnight lock-ins, adventurous outings (from canoeing to spelunking to amusement parks), and so forth all have a place in most youth groups. From a simple shared meal to a well-executed overnight trip, these events strengthen social bonds. Though not primarily ministry-oriented, often these events will help serve an evangelistic purpose as Christian young people are encouraged to invite their friends who do not follow Jesus, in hopes that they will make new friends and be exposed to the Christian culture of the larger group. Another key goal of social events is group bonding and strengthening friendships with those of a shared value system.

- *Personal contact.* A key component of youth ministry is the personal relationship(s) formed between the youth leader(s) and the young people themselves. This can take the form of one-to-one mentoring, leadership training in small groups, or simply congenial contact before and after youth meetings, in addition to many other settings. (We'll talk more about this in chapter 8, but responsible youth work must always take into account best practice regarding safeguarding, child protection, and background checks.) Personal relationships with young people can be more difficult in larger church or youth group settings, but it is my contention that modelling faithful walking with Jesus depends in large part on having some form of healthy, personal contact between faithful adults and young people. This applies not only to a salaried youth pastor, but also to volunteer youth leaders.

- *Small groups.* Some churches/youth groups may also have smaller groups that meet outside of the larger, regular gatherings or as breakout sessions within the main meeting. Not all youth groups have them, but they can be especially useful in larger churches or youth ministries where building community can be more challenging, due to the sheer numbers of youth involved, and/or the distance families travel to church. This is particularly true in megachurches. However, they are often utilized as part of a smaller gathering of young people. For instance, many in youth work have used small discussion groups as part of a larger teaching session. Small groups can also be a great way of utilizing young leaders and developing their gifts. They can also take the form of focused small groups with a special emphasis. These include things like leadership training, confirmation classes, worship band practice, drama teams, and a host of others.

- *Service and mission.* Lastly, many youth ministries will include some sort of emphasis on mission or serving. This could take the form of evangelistic efforts in the local community, volunteering in a nearby poverty ministry, visiting the elderly in a retirement home, or even an international and/or cross-cultural mission trip.

A little later, we're going to spend some time examining a form of youth ministry called "Attractional" youth ministry. It's a specific form of the traditional church youth group as outlined above, that is particularly dominant in larger churches, and especially megachurches and in urban and suburban areas. It has a huge following in American churches, but is also the dominant model of church-based youth ministry in the UK. It takes all of the above elements, but with the subtle, often unstated goal of *attracting* large numbers of young people into the church. As such, it also adds larger events, often with the goal of outreach or evangelism. We'll look into that more deeply in the next chapter, and affirm some aspects of this type of youth ministry, while also offering a firm critique of it. Attractional youth ministry is driven by the larger Church and its appeal and influence are widespread. Many smaller youth ministries rely heavily on attractional means, perhaps without realizing they are doing so.

Above, I made the claim that these six elements were almost universally present in the traditional church youth group, but now we need to qualify that. Because Christian youth groups often take on the personality, culture, and theology of the parent church/sponsoring organization – or indeed the personality of the youth worker – these elements will not necessarily be present in equal measure. For instance, some groups will place a high emphasis on pastoral care and personal relationship. The young people are loved, and have a real sense of belonging, but perhaps they are weak in discipleship. Other groups might emphasize the teaching of scripture, even to the point of stressing memorization, while there are few (or non-existent) opportunities for service. A well-balanced youth group will have a representation of all of the above elements, but their proportions will largely follow the theological emphasis of the parent church.

Youth Church

Although proponents of the Youth Church advocate it as a distinct youth ministry model, in my observation it is more or less the same as a traditional youth group (often with a strong Attractional emphasis), but with added religious language. Rather than a youth group, advocates refer to their group as a "youth church". Instead of having a "youth leader", a youth church would have a "youth pastor". In my limited observation, the differences are more or less semantic. Although seeking to have biblical and theological language to describe the efforts of such youth ministries should be applauded, the emphasis on language can also be a set-up for failure as it implies a sort of religious superiority over other Christian youth groups with similar goals. Furthermore, although I agree that young people following Jesus can be, and are in fact, part of the Church, it is problematic to imply that a Youth Church is an end in itself without the necessary inter-generational nature of the Church universal. There is a subtle danger that, instead of these groups *being* church, they could potentially be merely *mimicking* church. Furthermore, the Youth Church model by its very nature is often also Attractional, as it follows the patterns of the larger Church, and is often driven by the "bigger and better" motif. Visiting speakers, big stages, and light shows are often key ingredients to the Youth Church approach.

Detached Youth Work

Another youth work model that has gained traction in the United Kingdom is known as "detached youth work". The name comes from the location of this style of youth work, as it is done detached from any particular building or physical address. Youth work teams go out into areas where young people naturally congregate: parks and outdoor spaces, skate parks, sports facilities, town centres, street corners, and just about anywhere. The goal is to get to know young people, especially those who normally would not engage with other forms of church-based or Christian youth work. Pioneer youth worker Richard Passmore has written extensively about this type of youth work, having largely developed the approach while doing youth ministry in the Somerset market town of Chard, England.[3]

Whereas I am not aware of the practice of detached youth ministry in the United States, it has become a major method of youth engagement in the United Kingdom, and is also used by youth engagement teams that do not function out of the church or with specifically Christian purposes – in other words, secular youth work. In regards to Christian youth work, however, it is a praiseworthy model that is worth looking deeper into. A dear friend of mine led a detached youth work team in a suburban town for many years. She and her band of five to six volunteers would enter the town park on Friday evenings. The park, located in the middle of the town, would often see dozens of young people at the weekends. Many of the teens would engage in alcohol abuse, which would then fuel fights, or "youth on youth violence" as it is locally known. Judi's team would politely engage in conversation with any who were open to it, and offer support, prayer, pastoral counselling, and the like.

Why Do We Do it? Goals in Youth Ministry

Some readers may be truly surprised there are so many different ways to approach youth work, whereas others may think I've missed a model out. This is not meant to be an exhaustive list, just a quick overview and therefore a tool to aid us in our thinking about goals in youth ministry. For those who are just starting out, or looking to establish a model, where do you begin? Selecting and developing your youth ministry model will largely depend on several key factors: the culture and theology of your church or sponsoring organization; the local culture and context; and finally, the goal of your youth ministry. The goal will undoubtedly be formed and driven in large part by the other two factors.

As we stated above, one of the aims of this book is to help you think clearly and decisively about what you are doing in youth ministry, and why you are doing it. Perhaps you have been able to identify your work with young people as falling clearly into one of the above categories, or at least one more closely than the others. When was the last time you sat down with your youth ministry team (no matter how large or small) and talked about your goals for the youth ministry? This needs to be a semi-regular discussion that takes place – and the key members of your team should be able to articulate, with a reasonable degree of accuracy and understanding, what those goals are.

It is not my place here to tell you what those goals should be, as they will undoubtedly flow out of the theology and culture of your church or sponsoring organization, and also your local context. If you have not done so, it is worth setting aside a day or two for prayer and study, personal and/or group reflection, and brainstorming with the key players on your team to flesh out a purpose statement for your ministry to young people. Whom you invite to such a meeting will depend on your set-up. However, it will certainly need to involve a conversation (or perhaps multiple conversations) with your church leader or other supervisor, and any key team leaders in your ministry – whether volunteers or employees for whom you have oversight. Perhaps an all-day or even overnight retreat and brainstorming session is in order! Or otherwise, a few planning sessions on your own, followed up by some training meetings involving vision-casting and team-building around your model and long-term strategy. (It is advised to wait before planning such tactical sessions until after you've worked through this book, as we will be looking further into critiquing some of the above models, and also proposing a new one.)

In talking about goals and strategies in Christian youth work, there is a real danger in assuming the goals are obvious. Let me assure you they are not. Certainly church youth work will involve a number of theological and practical themes: evangelism, discipleship, service to others, equipping, community, calling/destiny, the glory of God, safety and safeguarding, etc. Nonetheless, how these themes are played out will vary greatly from setting to setting.

We have mentioned the need for your model to be in theological and cultural alignment with your church or sponsoring organization, but it will also need to factor in the local context. Contextualization is the process by which we live out the universal gospel in localized ways. Even though we serve the same Lord, a follower of Jesus in a remote village in South America will approach his journey with Christ in an entirely different way from an urban disciple from Sydney, Australia. Youth work will necessarily look entirely different in the two contexts. This is true not only across different continents, countries, and language barriers, but also within the same country from village to town to city. And even – I dare say – from one town or village to another. So often we see youth work models being set by the largest churches in the largest cities and towns of North America. The assumption is clear: "Since it worked for the 1st Saints Megachurch of Chicago, let's just do what they did and it will work here." However, simply copying what someone else has done is not recommended. In fact, it can be detrimental to effective witness among young people. In later chapters, we're going to illustrate more clearly the need for locally contextualized approaches to youth ministry.

What kind of context are you working in? Although we certainly need to take into account our country/national origin and language, we mean much more than this. Do you find yourself in an urban, suburban, large town, small town, or rural context? Even within urban contexts, there is a great deal of variation. Are you in a culturally diverse area? What ethnic groups are represented in your church, youth group, or target neighbourhood? What socio-economic factors are present? Is it primarily working class, middle class, working poor, wealthy, or a mix? We are not here trying to make a case for targeting any specific group, we are simply asking you to take note of what factors make up your ministry context. In my own experience of youth ministry, I have worked in a number of settings: a small church in a suburban college town, a megachurch in a large city with a metropolitan approach, an inner-city urban church (the first three all in the United States), and rural youth work in a village in England. Each of these settings required drastically different approaches to youth ministry.

Somewhat ironically, when my time was finished in the metropolitan megachurch setting, my next youth ministry assignment was the rural English village setting. Not only could I not simply copy what we had done in the American urban setting, I actually had to unlearn quite a few tactics, and assume I knew very little about youth ministry in this new setting. I had previously experienced having two employed staff serving with me, access to a large budget, and a database of around 200 young people. After moving to England, I was now the only employed youth worker, had a fraction of the ministry budget, and had roughly a dozen young people on the books. The most positive strategic step I took early on was assuming I knew nothing about youth ministry in the rural south of England. And, it was true – I didn't! This allowed me then to approach youth ministry as a student rather than an expert. We'll talk more about this attitude and posture later on as we delve into the Middle Space model.

It's easy to see a contextual difference between the rural village in South America and the urban church in Sydney. But what about micro-cultural differences? Are you able to recognize the ways your setting is different from the one fifteen miles down the road? The culture of both your church, and your local area, should be one of the first things you commit yourself to learning when you begin a new ministry post. In fact, I would argue that, if possible, one should not make any major changes to existing youth work without first taking a few months to learn as much as you can about the local context, church culture, and the key personalities and influencers in your local scene. In some cases, this may not be possible, as immediate changes are needed. This may be where a brand new work is starting, or a new facility is being utilized, or where radical changes are needed right off the bat, in order to comply with best practices. Nonetheless, even in these cases, extra time spent learning and soaking up all you can will never be time wasted, even if this appears to the casual observer to mean you are *not doing much.*

How Do We Do it?

Now that we've had a chance to think through the essence of youth ministry, as well as our stated goals, we can begin thinking about how we achieve them. It's time now to take a long, hard look at the model we have in place. Can you recognize your youth ministry in one of the models we've described above? If not, how would you describe the kind of youth ministry you do? What goals do you have for your youth ministry? Is the model you're using actively helping you to reach your goals? What challenges do you currently face in reaching your goals, and in what ways does your model either help or hinder you in the process? In youth ministry, we often refer to this combination as "best practice". Best practice occurs when what we do (our model and practices) aligns with why and how we do it (our goals and objectives), all the while taking into account our ethics, and the safety of those in our care, as well as our leadership team. When these three things come together – our model, goals, and ethics – it creates a holistic approach to youth ministry.

In the next chapter we're going to focus on critiquing what has become a dominant youth work model: the Attractional model. In particular, we'll look at the ways practitioners approach the sticky subject of outreach and evangelism. We'll then attempt to make a clear case for a new model altogether: Middle Space. However, before we do that, it's time to do some reflection. In each chapter, we'll have some questions for deeper reflection and discussion. I suggest completing these questions with your team and discussing your answers together. I hope you will find them a useful tool as you work to determine how to ensure best practice in youth ministry in your local context.

Reflection Section

What is your youth ministry model (from those we discussed above)? Describe it in three sentences or fewer.

What are the main goals of your youth work? (List no more than five.)

Are the key people on your team (volunteers or employed) able to articulate what you stated above? Are they even aware of it? If not, how could you change that? If yes, how have you achieved that?

Take it further. Ask a sample of your key volunteers what their understanding of your youth work model is. Don't press them for right or wrong answers. However, your findings should be very enlightening! Write down any insights you gained here.

What is the "local context" of your youth ministry (as discussed above)? How would you describe it in two to three sentences? Be sure to include geographical, demographical, cultural, and socio-economic identifiers.

2

Diagnosing the Problem

If there are so many models of youth ministry already in practice, why do we need another one? That is the question. Why this book, and why a new model for youth ministry? In this chapter, we hope to demonstrate the need for a new model of youth ministry based on a number of factors. First, our existing models are insufficient. There are massive, sweeping cultural changes happening across the Western world – and everywhere else – and our *modern* methods are outdated for ministry in a largely *postmodern* world. Second, the dominant model of church-based or congregational youth ministry, the Attractional model, has serious ethical shortcomings and ultimately falls short of being a faithful representation of the gospel of the kingdom. Third, our existing models do not offer an effective, ethically responsible, and biblically/theologically faithful model for doing youth evangelism.

There are many reasons why our current models are no longer sufficient as we move forward in the future. The task of youth ministry is significant: supporting young people through various aspects of their lives, making disciples of Jesus, providing pastoral counselling, and informal education. Western culture is in need of fresh paradigms of youth work. It is no longer enough to function in the role of a programme director or an events coordinator. Taking young people seriously necessarily means taking seriously a theological grounding for youth work.

After we've considered our goals for youth ministry (from the previous chapter), there are a few questions that need some attention:

- Is our youth ministry achieving what we set out to do?
- What is the long-term effect of youth ministry in general? And more specifically, what is the impact of *our* youth ministry?
- Are we equipping young people to keep following Jesus long after their time in the youth group has come and gone?
- How are we doing youth outreach and evangelism?

Again, it is not the purpose of this book to examine statistics and numbers in detail. Nonetheless, a brief look into the UK scene may illustrate the need for effective Christian youth work. Youth work practitioners in other national or regional contexts may want to examine statistics in their own countries to get a feel for the needs in their area.

The Need for a New Approach to Youth Ministry

"Gone are the days when Britain could be characterized undisputedly as a 'Christian country'."[4] So begins the book *The Faith of Generation Y*, which analyses five years of research with young people born roughly between 1982 and 2002. Although there is a deep Christian history in England, the reality is that only a small minority of people – roughly 10 per cent – attend church weekly, with another 10–15 per cent who are "fringe churchgoers" or "occasional churchgoers" attending only a few times per year, according to Tearfund (a Christian charity) research.[5] What is even more telling, however, is the large number of people who have no contact with the church whatsoever. According to the same study, "Two-thirds of UK adults (66 per cent) or 32.2 million people have no connection with church at present (nor with another religion)."[6] What strikes me about this is that if two-thirds of the UK population have no connection with church, then it is very possible that a large number of people also have no contact with devout Christians. Is it really possible that in the West (a region of the world with a rich connection to Christianity), a person can go through life without knowing a single devout Christian personally? If Tearfund's numbers are correct, then it is not only possible, but very likely. To make matters even worse, the Fourth English Church Census, conducted in 2005, found that on a typical Sunday, only 6.3 per cent of the English population were found in church.[7] Of this small number, only 5 per cent were eleven to fourteen years old, and a further 6 per cent were fifteen to nineteen years old.[8]

It appears that the English-speaking West is not only postmodern (more on this later), but perhaps also post-Christian. This is certainly true for England, and the USA seems to be heading in that direction as well. Kenda Creasy Dean's work in *Almost Christian*, dependent on the research of Smith and Denton in *Soul Searching*, illustrates how the dominant religion in the United States is no longer Christianity, but instead "Moralistic Therapeutic Deism",[9] which is the result of a sort of watered-down faith that has all the rough edges smoothed out in order to conform more easily with American culture. Dean's indictment is that it is not young people who are to blame, but adults in the Church who have failed to pass on to the next generation a Generative Faith.[10]

Although the cultural and historical developments in the United Kingdom are different from those in the United States, there are striking similarities. Smith and Denton's research showed that US young people were not actually averse to faith. Rather, they are simply apathetic towards it.[11] Our experience working with young people in England is similar. Upon moving here in 2008, I expected to encounter people who were hostile to the faith of the Church, but instead we found that, for most, issues of religion are just not part of their consciousness. While some Christian teens I know have experienced outright bullying for their Christian faith, most simply get puzzled expressions and questions. Their classmates simply cannot understand why they would want to be Christian. Religion is just not high on their priority list.

More recent research was undertaken by Youth for Christ in January of 2020 which shows trends moving in a more positive direction. Although their study acknowledges a lack of exposure to traditional religious structures and avenues of exposure to Christianity, the study also shows a surprising openness to spirituality, and even to Christianity. Thirty-six per cent of young people they spoke to said that if they were invited to learn more about God, they would be interested, an increase from 18 per cent in similar research undertaken in 2016 (just four years earlier)! Furthermore, young people seem to be much more open to the views of their Christian friends when presented with their views about Jesus: "51 per cent of the young people asked said that when their friends shared their views of Jesus with them that their own thoughts on God had been influenced."[12] These kinds of trends are always shifting and changing, and for the time being, there seems to be more openness to the person of Jesus than even just a few years ago.

We should make it very clear here that we are not simply talking about retention of young people as the goal of youth ministry. Andrew Root, in his social media posts and podcasts, rightly points out the insufficiency of such a goal, and the inevitable burnout and disillusionment from youth workers themselves when keeping 'bums in pews' becomes the main driving force of Christian youth work.

A question we all need to be asking ourselves is, "Why is youth ministry important?" If the above statistics and descriptions of life in a post-Christian society are not enough to get us thinking about the importance of youth ministry, then I refer you back to my story. My own story and testimony are intimately connected to my vocation in youth ministry. Having grown up with a pained view and experience of fathers, I was nurtured by fathers in the church, and ultimately by God himself. How could I ensure that fathering would continue to take place in the churches I hoped to serve? But even more to the point, what about those young people who did not have the benefit of a supporting and welcoming church family? How could I expose more of them to that love and empowerment that I – and so many of you reading this book – have experienced?

The Problems of Attractional Youth Ministry

I spent just under three years serving as the Student Minister of a large metropolitan church in the United States. Our youth ministry had all the essential elements of the standard church youth group: regular meetings, camps and retreats, social events, and personal contact, as well as small groups and opportunities for service and mission. The church, while located in an urban setting, is not an inner-city church. Rather, it is a metropolitan church. A locally focused inner-city church might be tucked away in a neighbourhood ministering to the needs of the local community. Such a church can respond to the call of God in their localized setting, bearing witness to Jesus Christ in tangible ways. By contrast, a metropolitan church will generally be on the intersection of a major road or highway, visible to drivers who pass by. Rather than meeting local needs, it seeks to draw in people from greater distances.

The church where I worked is by all definitions a megachurch (definitions of the term vary, but we are generally defining it here as a congregation with more than 1,000 people in total attendance). At the time of my service there, the church had over 9,000 members, and most Sundays would see around 3,500 in attendance. The youth group on a Sunday morning or Wednesday evening could see in excess of 100 young people. It doesn't take a lot of discernment to note the disparity between the number of regular church attendees and the comparatively small number of youth group attendees. Those who attended the youth group – roughly aged eleven to eighteen – by these numbers accounted for only 3 per cent of the total number in attendance, which is disproportionate even by conservative statistics. In this particular setting, it seemed that the goal of youth ministry was not journeying with young people on the walk of faith, nor even making disciples among young people. Youth ministry was simply a tool, a cog in the larger wheel. *Good* youth ministry served as an attraction for parents and families into the larger church. Simply stated, youth ministry was a driver for church growth.

Before we offer a further critique of the model of ministry in place among the congregation, it is worth saying a few positive things. We encountered some wonderful families in our time there. There were parents doing amazing discipleship of their own children. There were young people truly serving God and doing amazing things in his name. For instance, one of my former youth group members was a lovely girl called Betty. Betty, the teenage daughter of Ethiopian immigrants to the USA, had become passionate about the injustice of human trafficking, so she decided to do something about it. In one single fundraising event, she raised over $10,000 in aid of organizations fighting human trafficking. Other former members are missionaries in Asia, singer-songwriters serving as witnesses in popular music, worship pastors, teachers, as well as real-estate agents and workers in other secular jobs.

Another positive thing about large churches: a large church in an affluent area means a large budget. As most youth pastors will attest, having a generous budget for youth ministry means more funds for teaching materials, help with transportation to summer camp, bigger and better events, technological aids for communication, and so forth. It means the ability to hire more staff to help minister to young people.

Let's take a deeper look now at what we mean by the Attractional megachurch model of youth ministry. Our critique is based on three factors: the struggle to build community; its events-driven and numbers-oriented nature; and finally the fact that it is based on not only an inadequate model of youth ministry, but an inadequate model of church.

Our metropolitan megachurch was largely a commuter church. Set within the city limits of Atlanta, the majority of attendees drove in from nearby – or not-so-nearby – suburbs. In many ways, this reflects the culture of the Atlanta Metro area in general. It is known for its sprawling suburbs and resulting horrible traffic. Let's say that a family lives a half-hour drive away, north of the church. Another family lives a half-hour drive away, south of the church. Both families have teenagers in the youth group. We now have teenagers who live an hour away from each other, but attend the same church and youth group, go on retreats together, and are trying to follow Jesus together. They go to different schools, live in different communities, and come from completely different demographic areas (ethnically, socio-economically, and micro-culturally). The challenge to build community was very real. To further the point, it is worth noting that this is a moderately conservative example, as I knew several young people who were connected to the youth ministry who lived 45 minutes' drive away in either direction, thus stretching the driving distance between these young people to an hour and a half! What does pastoral visitation look like in that setting? What about the prospect of offering support or interaction to local schools or youth organizations? We would have had more than thirty schools represented in our youth group.

Problematically, youth ministry in this type of setting becomes necessarily events-driven. This was an accepted assumption within our pastoral staff team. The assumption wasn't questioned, nor was the statement altered to, "Youth ministry *in this church* is events-driven." It was merely assumed that effective youth ministry was based around putting on successful events. What is meant by this statement is this: successful youth ministry is based on planning and executing a variety of events, which are used to draw in or *attract* large numbers of young people with the end goal of reaching these young people with the gospel. The bigger and better the event, the more likely young people are to attend, and therefore the more likely they are to hear and respond to the gospel. At a casual glance, there is a logic here that makes sense. Any Christian youth worker wants more young people to follow Jesus, and if events contribute to that, then putting on more and/or better events makes sense.

There are some inherent problems with this assumption, however. Events-driven youth ministry is based on the faulty assumption that bigger is always better. Although Jesus wanted his disciples to catch more fish, it was not the calibre of the nets that was instrumental in their large catch, but rather their obedience to the lordship of Jesus in casting their nets on the other side. Jesus didn't instruct his disciples to go out and build the biggest boats that Galilee had ever seen, decorate them with gold and silver ornaments, jewels, and chandeliers. They didn't spend millions on the latest equipment – fishing lures that would attract fish to practically jump in the boat of their own accord. Nor was he trying to get them to attract even more fish from other lakes and streams farther away, where the fish would have to swim for miles and miles just to be near the Attractional Mega-boat. I'm being a bit ridiculous here, but hopefully you see my point.

We read in the Gospels of the masses following Jesus, and I am encouraged by the multitudes who wanted to be near him. However, we also read of them turning away from following him when it became clear that the demands of the gospel were more stringent than they first imagined.

Another problem with events-driven youth ministry is practical in nature. A successful, Attractional youth event – to be effective for communicating the gospel – requires an avenue for follow-up with attendees. In my previous youth work, we once hosted a video game event. We had obtained the addresses of households within a certain radial distance from the church who had teenagers within our target age range. We then invited them to a video game tournament based on then-current gaming trends. The prize for the winning team would be a brand new gaming system, which was at that time the latest version of the Xbox. The event was much more successful, in terms of numbers, than we could have imagined. Roughly 200 young people entered the tournament and very few of them – less than 10 per cent – were members of the church youth group.

The problem then became how to follow up with them. The event itself was not explicitly evangelistic. We had not planned a "bait-and-switch" event, a common youth work tactic wherein young people are invited to an event under a false premise (free food or some fun activity being the most common draws) without any explanation of the spiritual nature of said event, and subsequently preached at while the doors are locked and no one can escape! Although such tactics are common, they are (in this writer's opinion) highly unethical. They are disingenuous, lacking integrity regarding the gospel message – which must first be lived out, and then shared openly and graciously – but also regarding the relationships with the young people themselves. They are akin to being invited to a friend's house for dinner, only to arrive and find out that the dinner was a ploy to get you signed up for a multilevel marketing scheme.

So how do you follow up after a largely successful (in terms of numbers) youth event? Logically, the answer is often to plan another event. In our case, we had an all-night lock-in planned for a few weeks later. The lock-in brought as many young people as the gaming event did. In fact, we had so many young people that we did not have enough transportation for the different phases of the all-nighter. One of the most horrifying experiences of my youth ministry in that setting was the feeling of fear and dread when I saw the queue of young people waiting to get in the door and the realization that we were not prepared to receive them all. The only thing worse was that, again, we did not have an adequate follow-up plan.

As we've hinted at already, the problem of Attractional ministry is not unique to youth work. In fact, those of us who have tried Attractional techniques have likely picked them up from the larger church. Alan Hirsch describes the problem well in regards to church growth: "[To] grow a contemporary church following good church-growth principles, there are several things you must do and constantly improve on." The last of the seven tasks is, "Make sure that next week is better than the previous week, to ensure that the people keep attending."[13] The emphasis on bigger and better applies to Attractional youth work just as well as to church growth.

In this model, very often the question becomes, "What event can we put on that will get the largest amount of young people through the door?" In some ways, this is a noble aim. More young people coming to a church event is a good thing, right? But in other ways it falls short. Even if you can get 200 young people through the door who do not follow Jesus, what happens next? What is the plan for follow-up and follow-through? But even more important is a question of the meaning of evangelism: at what point does "evangelism" simply boil down to an event that we put on, as opposed to a lifestyle of faithfulness to the expression and procla-mation of the love of God and the cause of the kingdom?

In addition to being inherently events-driven, another problem with this particular youth ministry model is that it is also numbers-oriented. In fact, to be events-driven *necessarily* means to be numbers-driven. Even if church leadership claims it is not about numbers (as I often overheard in pastoral staff meetings at my megachurch), events-driven youth ministry is certainly about getting large numbers of young people through the doors. Once again, we may wish to clarify that seeing large numbers of young people come to faith in Jesus is indeed a noble goal. However, we must also ask the question, at what expense is this goal achieved? Which is better: a large number of young people who believe in Jesus but have a very shallow, lifeless faith? Or a small group of teenagers following Jesus with devotion and faithfulness? I will not attempt to answer the question, as both of these choices have merits. The problem, however, with events-driven, numbers-oriented youth ministry is that by failing to entertain the question it results in the former scenario over against the latter. Issues of quality, faithfulness, longevity, and perseverance are not often raised in settings where numbers are clearly the priority.

A further question remains as well. By placing the emphasis on the number of young people coming to an event, we are assuming that those large numbers are being "impacted by the gospel". But what if they aren't? What if they're coming for any number of other reasons – they like the music, the events are fun, their friends come, a cute boy/girl goes there – what if simply showing up isn't the same as being impacted by the gospel?

We must come to an important theological, or more specifically ecclesiological (theology of the Church) critique of the Attractional youth ministry model, and that is this. It is an inadequate model of youth ministry because it is based on an inadequate model of church: the Attractional church model. The Attractional church model says, "If you build it, they will come."[14] As noted above, the Attractional youth ministry focuses on bigger and better events in order to draw in large numbers of young people. This makes the prospect of building genuine community, affected by healthy and nurturing relationships, incredibly difficult. It is difficult by virtue of the distance people travel to come to the bigger, better church, but also by virtue of the sheer number of young people involved and, therefore, the large number of adult volunteers and leaders needed to run the ministry.

In spite of the large numbers of young people that came into contact with the ministry at the megachurch where I worked, there was a disparaging gap in the number of teens involved in the youth ministry, when compared with the number of attendees in church on any given week (as noted above). Why was less than 3 per cent of the congregation on a Sunday made up of those between the ages of eleven and eighteen? Statistically and demographically, surely the number of people in the age group described should have been higher than that. There are a number of possible ways to explain the disparity. It is possible that there were teenagers present in church that did not, for whatever reason, engage in the youth ministry. Although I know this to be true, we did not have access to any statistics that would have given us helpful numbers to indicate it. Another possibility is that teenagers in many families simply did not attend church with their parents. We are considering a situation in the United States, yet it is interesting to note that in many churches in the United Kingdom, it is assumed that teenagers will stop attending church at a certain point in their adolescence (usually between the ages of fourteen and eighteen), and it is my contention that parents often inadvertently encourage this.

As we move forward into proposing a new model of youth ministry, we will continue to critique aspects of Attractional youth work, as points of contrast. For now, we must make one final case for our new model.

Attractional Youth Ministry and Evangelism

There is a bigger missiological (theology of mission) problem with Attractional youth ministry, in turn, creating a theological issue. How does an events-driven, numbers-oriented, Attractional youth ministry do evangelism and mission? The quick answer is obvious: hold evangelistic events and provide service/mission opportunities for young people. But is this adequate? I contend it is not. Evangelism, by definition, is sharing the Good News. Events can help facilitate sharing the Good News, but making evangelism out to *be* an event is problematic at best. The process of making disciples out of young people will most certainly involve teaching them how to share the Good News of Jesus with their friends, but in the Attractional church model, evangelism is something that happens at church. Professional ministers are the ones who communicate the gospel – it is what they are paid to do. Too often, young people in traditional youth ministries (at the megachurch and smaller church alike) are taught simply to invite their friends to the next big youth ministry event, with the hopes that the friend will catch enough of the Good News and get saved. However, how many young people are taught about lifestyle evangelism, relational evangelism, or bringing Jesus to their friends as opposed to simply bringing their friends to the church youth group?

Not only does event-based evangelism hinder the discipleship process of young people themselves, it also limits the evangelism opportunities for those in full-time ministry. While I was youth minister at the megachurch, so much of my own time was spent in my office, within the walls of the church building. All of those events weren't going to plan themselves! There was paperwork to do, forms to fill in, transportation to arrange, budget requests to be made, teaching/sermons to write and prepare. I went into youth ministry largely because I wanted to share Jesus with young people. Although I was doing that with those who were already coming to church, I had very little time for interacting with people outside of church. Because I commuted to work in typical Atlanta traffic, I spent roughly two hours a day driving. I worked some evenings and most weekends. I barely knew my neighbours. Any personal evangelism efforts I made had to be done on my own time, of which I had very little!

Nonetheless, young people were, in fact, coming to Christ. At camps and retreats, and through the youth ministry, teenagers were coming to faith in Jesus. However, those young people who were getting saved were largely coming from homes with Christian backgrounds. To put it another way, they were getting saved off of the church pews. A niggling thought began to grow in the back of my mind: these young people were probably going to find faith eventually, regardless of whether I was doing the youth work there or not.

I want to be clear that this is not simply a rant against large churches. There are some great things about large churches: a wealth of wonderful people, lots of creativity, and large budgets, to name a few. These are all things that generally make youth pastors smile. Our critique here is specifically of Attractional youth ministry. It's true that large churches have spearheaded this model, so there is some overlap. However, is it possible for some large churches to be using other, healthier models of church and youth ministry? Certainly! If not a critique of large churches in general, neither is it merely an airing of past grievances. I look back on my time in Atlanta with great fondness and we are still in regular communication with a number of friends we made while there.

I was never going to be able to last very long in a leadership role in a church where I was becoming increasingly disillusioned with the ministry model in place. I lasted almost three years at our metropolitan megachurch. When and why did I leave? Near the end of my third year in post, I attended a leadership conference, pioneered by a former mentor of mine. At the conference, there was a recurring theme around church planting (in other words, starting a new church) and other apostolic forms of ministry and outreach. By "apostolic" here, we simply mean having an emphasis on *mission*. An "apostle" is someone sent by the Lord to do a specific task. Apostolic ministry is characterized by mission, innovation, and trying new things.

This conference served as a turning point for my wife and me, both in terms of us moving away from my role at the megachurch, but also in terms of guiding us to think and plan ministry in new and strategic ways. It was at this conference that I was introduced to the ideas of churches as "missional communities" (more on that in chapter 5). Just a few months later, I resigned from my post. I had been growing continually frustrated by events-driven youth ministry where the aim seemed to be getting more bodies through the door. I was also finding it frustrating that 99 per cent of my interaction with other people was with people who were already Christians. I began asking myself some hard questions. Although young people in the youth ministry were coming to Christ, they were coming from Christian families. Where were the converts from non-Christian backgrounds? In fact, where was a Christian youth pastor in a megachurch even going to interact meaningfully with teenagers from atheist, agnostic, Muslim, Hindu, or other backgrounds? There didn't seem to be much time for developing those sorts of relationships. If I was going to do relational evangelism, it would have to be on my own time. I was still attending hardcore punk and heavy metal concerts, and trying to make contacts in that way, but with a young family and a full-time ministry inside of church walls, that was becoming more difficult.

The idea of church planting became something I could not easily shake. In my personal prayer times and reading of scripture, I began to question heavily the ways we were doing ministry. Scripturally, there was one phrase that really began to compel me: "Jesus, friend of sinners". I began to see the phrase "friend of sinners" not as an insult, as some of Jesus' enemies would have intended, but rather as an aspiration. The term "sinners" served as a sort of code word to identify those people out there who are not as holy as us. The people who don't believe, or behave, or dress the way we do. The problem for me was that I spent so much time within church walls that I didn't know any "sinners". I had no time, nor any means to get to know people outside my profession in the church where I served. Yet the description of Jesus as the Friend of Sinners haunted me. It seemed like it would be an honour to have this intended derogatory phrase hurled at me too. When I initially resigned my youth ministry position, it was with a view to planting a church that would deliberately target working with non-Christians. Even though that specific goal never materialized in the way I once thought it would, I include the detail here for a significant reason. Middle Space youth work draws heavily on apostolic, church-planting ideas – particularly that of "missional communities".

Too often youth ministry in the United States is based on the outdated and problematic Attractional model. We have specifically critiqued the model found at one metropolitan megachurch in the southern part of the United States. At this point, it might be tempting to write off this whole critique with, "We're not a megachurch." Or something similar. But herein lies the problem. The Attractional youth ministry model is so pervasive that it has taken root in most Evangelical, Pentecostal, and Mainline Protestant churches to the degree that many (most?) of them follow the same model. This is especially true in the United States, and there are large swathes of this influence in the United Kingdom and elsewhere as well.

So why a new model of youth ministry? It is time to consider an alternative approach to youth ministry that takes both discipleship and mission seriously.

Reflection Section

In what ways have you seen Attractional youth ministry at work, either in your own youth work or elsewhere?

What positive or negative aspects of Attractional ministry have you encountered?

At the beginning of the chapter, we asserted that current models of youth ministry are insufficient for contemporary youth work. Do you agree with this assessment? Why or why not?

3

How Do We Do Evangelism In Youth Ministry?

I have a confession to make. Even though I know one should never make assumptions – especially in regards to ministry – I am making a huge assumption about the readers of this book. I am assuming that most of you have experienced, observed, or been affected by Attractional ministry models in some way. Even if you're deliberately working within a distinctly different model (Refuge/Safe Space, Specialized, or Detached), you will have been impacted by Attractional approaches to ministry, if only because you've chosen to avoid them. The Attractional model, for many reasons, has become one of the most dominant and/or influential models of youth ministry in the Western world. Although the reasons for this are too complex to analyse here, this is largely due to the cultural influence of the American megachurch and suburban large church approaches to ministry. It seems that the perfect storm of post-industrial consumerism, rugged individualism, and free-market capitalism combined with popular theology have led to churchgoers becoming consumers of a product, rather than members of a family. I wouldn't be too surprised if we started seeing "drive-thru" church services coming soon to a suburban neighbourhood near you. "Thank you for coming to McChurch, how can I provide you with an excellent religious experience today?", "Hi, thanks. Could I please get a short sermon, heavy on inspiration and light on conviction, please?"

Though he does not use the term *attractional*, *The Message* writer Eugene Peterson offers a scathing critique of the approach in his book *Five Smooth Stones for Pastoral Work*, where he claims, "Advertising techniques, promotional budgets, and organizational charts are bagatelles in [pastoral] work. They are, it is argued, useful tools to assist the pastoral work. In fact they are enormous distractions. They absorb, like sponges, the energies that ought to go into prayer; they dilute concentration in worship; they clutter preaching."[15] Peterson's comments, while addressing modern approaches to pastoral ministry in the wider church, are relevant for our discussion of youth work, since more often than not, church-based youth work follows the theology and ethos of the sponsoring church or organization.

As we've spent some time already looking at the problems of Attractional youth work, and especially its all-too-common reliance on event-based evangelism efforts, let's look at other ways of doing youth evangelism. Before proceeding below, maybe take two to three minutes to think about your own youth ministry approach to evangelism. How do you do it? We'll leave some more time at the end of this chapter to reflect more thoroughly on your evangelism model, so don't spend too much time critiquing yours for now; just try to identify what you do and how you do it, as succinctly as possible.

For all of us who are followers of Jesus, one thing is clear: someone told us about the love of God. Someone explained to us the Good News of Jesus. How did that happen for you? Do you remember when you became a Christian, or what the factors were that led up to that point?

It's safe to say, that across the readers of this book, we'll have dozens of different ways that people came to Christ. It is also my assumption (there's that word again!) that most of us who are interested in Christian youth work want young people to know the joy and love of following Jesus. So how do we get that message across? There are at least four different ways youth ministries and churches approach youth evangelism.

Event-based Evangelism

As we've stated above, Attractional youth ministry relies almost entirely on events. So far, we've been fairly critical of event-based ministry in general, and especially when it comes to evangelism or sharing the Good News. At the same time, we don't want to overlook some potentially positive contributions in this regard. Sharing God's love and message of forgiveness is a privilege, and reducing it to a single event focused on numbers misses the mark. However, it also should not be overlooked that there is a fair bit of innovation in creating such occasions. In addition to the video game tournaments and overnight lock-ins we described above, a vast array of different events might be considered in Attractional youth work. These events generally fall into one of a number of categories, with some degree of overlap.

Social Events

Specially designed social events are often utilized as a way to get young people to invite their friends. This can include barbecues, pizza parties, and other food-related events, as well as lock-ins, spectator sports, picnics in the park, and loads more. But we're not just talking about get-togethers. For social events to take on an evangelistic bent, there needs to be some level of strategic intentionality in regards to sharing the gospel message. Either this will be with the intention of building relationships with young people who don't know Jesus, or there might be some sort of "God talk" at the event, generally pitched at a very basic level.

An additional level of impact can be achieved by taking a social event, as above, and turning it into an adventure or physical challenge, thus adding an opportunity for liminality. These can range from hiking or biking trips to camping and backpacking, river rafting, etc. The nature of the challenge will depend on what is available in the nearby geographic region, the strengths and abilities of the youth leaders and volunteers, and the nature of the young people themselves (age, size, physical and mental fortitude, etc.).

Spiritual Events

By spiritual events here, we mean those occasions specifically designed to engage with spiritual matters. These might include special youth services, sometimes called "youth rallies" (or some other term), where there is some type of talk or other gospel presentation. These events can be held in local churches, but often they are mass events designed to draw in hundreds or even thousands of young people. Although these events can be effective tools for exposing young people to the gospel message (when combined with an Invitational approach – more on that below), there is a subtle, but very real danger here as well. Big events can easily create an emotionally hyped environment. There might be a worship band with loud music, a stage and light show, or a big-name speaker (to Christians anyway). All of these in and of themselves are fine in one sense. However, the Good News of God's reign in Jesus Christ is much more than emotional manipulation. How many young people (or adults for that matter) have put their hand up or walked down the aisle to receive Jesus, only to fall away a few weeks or months later because there was no real or lasting commitment to the faith? It is not our purpose here to provide an exhaustive critique of large evangelistic events, as much as to critique an over-reliance on events of *any* kind as the sole means of sharing the gospel.

Musical/Artistic Events

Although the trend seems to have died down in recent years, in previous decades a major stream of youth evangelism involved concerts and other musical events. Although similar in some ways, these events are distinct from those highlighted above in that they are marketed and promoted as concerts. Step one: hire a professional Christian rock or rap group (or whatever other genre was popular at the time). Step two: promote the event across the town/region. Step three: get your youth group kids to invite their friends, and most likely downplay the Christian-ness of the event. Step four: it's concert time! After the hall is filled with young people, lock the doors and preach the gospel to them in contemporary lingo.

Of course, there is nothing inherently wrong with Christian concerts or arts events. Just as human relationships are inherently valuable and meaningful, so are the creative arts inherently valuable and meaningful. God the Creator – Father, Son, and Holy Spirit – created us in his own image and after his likeness. There is something about us that is truly like God. Theologians and philosophers call this "ontology", or the study of what it means *to be*. We are created by and for relationship with God and others. We are also created to create. When we channel those artistic inclinations, we are acting in ways that resemble our God the Creator. Music in particular is a powerful tool of communication. Not in spite of this, but because of it, we must use it wisely. Communication and human expression through music are intrinsically valuable, but let's steer clear of anything manipulative.

* * *

I must turn again to confession. As a man who has served as a youth worker/youth pastor/youth minister in various locations, I have taken part in all of the above. Every last one of them. There are some good things about all of these methods, and some not so good. Who doesn't love a good pizza party, or a backpacking weekend with the lads/ladies, or a great concert? Using these tools to build relationships can be time and money well spent, not only because relationships are often key to effectively sharing the gospel, but also because there is something deeply theological and foundational to human relationships. It is clear from the Garden of Eden, right in the beginning of the Bible, that we humans were made for relationship. Everything God made in the early chapters of Genesis is described with the words, "it was good." When he made humanity, however, an extra emphasis was added: "it was *very* good" (Genesis 1:31). And yet even with all the goodness of creation and the very-goodness of humanity, there was still one thing that was not good: "It is not good for the man to be alone" (Genesis 2:18). We were made for relationships – meaningful connections with other human beings.

It is no surprise, then, that sharing the gospel largely rests on relationships. I asked you earlier if you remembered when or how you first became a Christian. I'd venture to say that 95 per cent of us could point to a key relationship that played a significant part: a friend who invited us to church or youth group, a praying grandparent, a mother or father, a youth worker who explained the gospel to us, or another role model who emulated what it was like to walk with Jesus. The problem with event-based evangelism is that it reduces sharing the gospel to a single event. No matter how big our ministry budget is, how bright the stage lights are, how tasty the pizza is, there is no replacement for real, genuine, authentic relationships.

Even here there is a danger that the relationship becomes a means to an end, rather than an end in itself. As Christians we rightly criticize "situational ethics" and "ends justify the means" mentalities, but if not careful we can be guilty of the same tactics in regard to evangelism. The Bible is clear that relationships are important and valuable, full stop. Young people deserve our authentic love and support because they are loved and valued by God, not just because they are projects we are working on. As my World Missions professor, Ridley Usherwood, used to say, "They have names, not just souls."

These events and others like them are often guilty of the tried and untrue "bait and switch" tactic we mentioned earlier. The unsuspecting victim is invited to the party, with no mention of it being a Christian event, or at least not a true representation of it, and then the goalposts are switched once they've arrived. About ten years ago, I was driving some young people to the legendary UK youth festival, Soul Survivor. One of the teenage girls in my youth group had invited a friend to come along. During the drive, Emily (names changed) asked what we were going to be doing, so I started telling her about the worship, the talks, and the seminars. She had a slightly confused look on her face when Charlotte (who had invited her) butted in, "It's more like a music festival." Although Charlotte had taken a bold step by inviting Emily along to the festival, she had not been forthright with her about what the event was all about; it was a massive four-day event designed to help young people get to know Jesus better. Although we might fault Charlotte for not being as bold in her witness as we might hope, we youth workers are often guilty of the same offence when we advertise an event to young people with hidden or ulterior motives.

Is it possible to do event-based evangelism well? To do it without violating serious ethical boundaries? I suppose it might be possible, if we take into account the above critiques. Let's look at another positive aspect of evangelistic events: the role of the young person. Using such events as evangelistic efforts relies, in large part, on the willingness of young people to invite their friends to take part, especially their friends who are not Christians. As such, they rely on an *Invitational* evangelism style. Lee Strobel and Mark Mittelberg, in their book *Becoming a Contagious Christian: Youth Edition*,[16] identify six different evangelism styles, and they argue for the importance of identifying one's evangelism style. Individuals in the Invitational style might not feel comfortable confronting their friends with the claims of the gospel, or praying for supernatural intervention from God for a specific need in their life. Sometimes, it is thought that all some young people need to offer is an invitation to a Christian event.

Although I applaud thinking outside the box in regard to the task of sharing one's faith, it is likely that events-driven approaches rely too heavily on the invitational tactics of young people. Involving young people in evangelism is praiseworthy, but if the young people's only role in evangelism is inviting their friends to an event where they can hear a talk or sermon by a youth speaker, it seems we're leaving too much in the hands of "professionals". There is a real danger here in that while trying to empower our young people to share Jesus with their friends through invitation, we are actually diminishing their role in sharing Jesus.

We would like to be very clear here in affirming *any* genuine attempt at sharing the gospel. Lots of effort, time, money, and other resources have been poured into creating events in the hopes of using them to expose more people to the transforming love of God. But we also want to be equally clear in critiquing the absurd notion that this can be boiled down to a single event. Jesus called twelve men to follow him wherever he went and do what he did. Let this be our model for relationship-building and transformational gospel-sharing.

Peer Evangelism

Another common approach to youth evangelism is by peer evangelism. By this, we simply mean equipping and empowering our young people to tell others about Jesus. In many ways, this is a fantastic approach. Who better to tell young people about Jesus than other young people who have met and grown to love the living Lord? As an adult, I often struggle to find ways to share Jesus with young people. I know they need to hear about God's love for them. I also know I have a responsibility (a joyful one, but a responsibility nonetheless) to share the gospel with others, including young people. However, the logistics alone create an ethical conundrum. How does a grown man approach young people to talk to them about God without creating all sorts of cringe factors? When we consider the difficulty of a youth worker, who is employed by a church to do youth ministry, in building and maintaining relationships with teens who don't know Jesus, we uncover a logistical nightmare and a potentially difficult safeguarding situation. Considering the above, it seems like empowering our Christian teens to share Jesus with their friends is the most logical solution.

Empowering young people to share Jesus with their friends is *always* a good idea, for many reasons. First, it is a vital part of their own discipleship journey. Learning to be Christian necessarily involves learning to tell others about the love of God and how his goodness has impacted our own lives. Too many adults have never learned how to be an effective witness for Christ. Just a few weeks ago someone in their seventies, who has been a Christian for decades, admitted to me, "I just don't know what to say." If we can reverse those kinds of trends by teaching people from a young age, then all the better. When combined with an Invitational approach (as described above), it can be particularly effective.

There are, however, some problems with utilizing peer evangelism as the primary or only method of youth evangelism. The biggest one is this: how do we, as adult youth workers, model sharing the faith if we are only equipping young people to do it? The problem is not primarily a didactic (teaching) problem, but one of our own integrity. Let me put it another way: are we asking young people to do something that we are not doing ourselves? When I was working in the United States, this question really got under my skin. Like so many other youth pastors, I was encouraging my young people to share their faith with their friends, and to invite them to events at our church or sponsored by our youth group. But in my own private life, I had virtually no significant relationships with anyone who didn't believe in Jesus as the way, the truth, and the life. Why? All my time was spent at church. I was working long hours as a youth pastor, commuting an hour to/from work each day, and had no time to interact significantly with my neighbours. How was I, as a full-time Christian youth minister, to come into contact with non-Christians? How was I to build significant friendships with them? In short, was I getting my young people to do my work for me?

Detached Approaches

We have looked at Detached[17] youth work briefly above; here we want to focus on the contributions that Detached youth work methods bring to youth evangelism. We're not necessarily trying to do an in-depth survey of Detached youth work, as much to see what kind of youth evangelism methods take place *out there*, so to speak. That is, sharing the gospel of Jesus outside of church settings. We'll include here various methods of evangelism, including both Detached youth work and so-called "old-school" methods of evangelism, simply because they both take place outside of normal church settings. This might involve things like street witnessing, door-to-door evangelism, and similar techniques. Even though the long-term goals and methods of these models may be vastly different, we include them both here to talk about both the prospects and the problems of doing evangelistic work (of any sort) in non-sacred spaces.

Detached youth work, and particularly Symbiotic youth work,[18] carry the very noble and commendable task of journeying with young people. They are not setting out to make conversions as much as to get to know young people, and then to go together to new places spiritually and religiously, perhaps even creating new forms of church. Even though the model is not about "cold-turkey" evangelism, its very essence is evangelistic. Getting to know young people in the hope of journeying together towards Jesus – what is more gospel-centric than that?

On the other end of the Detached spectrum are the old-school methods of witnessing: street evangelism, door-to-door witnessing, etc. In street ministry, youth ministers and young people alike meet together and canvass the streets – usually in urban areas – armed with Bibles and evangelistic tracts, starting up conversations with strangers on the street. They might start by asking a provocative question, like, "If you died tonight, would God let you into heaven?" Other, slightly less intrusive examples might be used instead. For instance, "Do you think there is an afterlife?" The door-to-door method is very similar, except that instead of walking the streets, practitioners knock on doors in a particular neighbourhood or housing estate. Another method is to invite people to come to an event, usually later that evening or later during the week. The event might be a block party, youth event, or evangelistic rally at a nearby church.

Despite their controversial nature – even amongst Christians, people tend to love or hate them – there is a lot to be said for such methods. It takes an extraordinary amount of bravery and boldness to walk up to a total stranger and attempt a conversation about spiritual matters. One can question how effective these methods are, but let's at least recognize how committed to the gospel one has to be to attempt such a task! Additionally, street evangelism and detached work accomplish something that our other methods do not: they focus on engaging with people who may not otherwise interact with the Church. Events-driven and peer-based youth evangelism both assume at least some connection to the church, even if that connection is merely a young person who is already a part of your group. Street witnessing and its related forms attempt to target those who might otherwise have no connection to the faith.

Although there are certainly some positive aspects to Detached evangelism methods, there are some problems as well. The first objection we have is its unpredictable nature. Although taking the message to the streets is indeed noble, the variety of settings means that it is next to impossible to control the environment. This could lead to some dangerous scenarios. I am not against putting oneself in harm's way for the sake of the gospel when it is appropriate, but the truth is that it may not always be what's best for our young people. The unpredictable element also then includes things like variations in the weather. Not only would it be unpleasant to do witnessing when it's pouring down with rain, but also you're unlikely to find anyone willing to engage in a conversation in those conditions.

Our second objection is related to this idea of engagement. We said above that even amongst committed Christians, there is a huge divide over utilizing these direct approaches to witnessing. Some love it (or at least admire it), whereas others hate it. I have concluded that much of this comes down to one's personality and/or spiritual gifts and personal make-up. In essence, street evangelism appeals to a certain type of personality. Your typical door-to-door witnessing enthusiast will typically be an extrovert. They will likely be comfortable with confrontation and/or argument and debate. They will be the type not to get discouraged by hearing "no, thank you" 100 times before getting that one person who is willing to talk. *Becoming a Contagious Christian* refers to this evangelism style as the Direct style. But the fact that this style is only one of the six styles identified in the book tells us something: it's not for everyone.

It probably won't come as a surprise to you that I have engaged in street evangelism and door-to-door ministry. Although I have enjoyed the thrill of stepping out of my comfort zone, I must admit I have often questioned the effectiveness of it. I don't really enjoy it when a stranger knocks on my door to try to sell me windows, or to talk to me about their religion, or to buy any spare gold I have lying around (as if a church youth worker has "spare gold" anyway!). I'll open my door to a neighbour any time – they might need to borrow something, or perhaps they're inviting me out for a drink! But a stranger at the door always makes me roll my eyes and keep the door halfway closed. How much more sceptically do people in the streets or in their homes react to us when we want to talk to them about a God they may or may not even believe in!

This leads us to our final question about Detached evangelism methods: are they valid? By this we mean a number of things. Are they outdated methods? Are they really appropriate? It seems that some of the ethical questions we raised above with other methods apply here. For instance, if the sharing of the gospel requires a depth of relation-ship, then certainly that calls into question witnessing to total strangers. Another question involves the nature of said conversations. There are some decent conversation starters, but also some really poor ones. It's my opinion that the really in-your-face approaches like, "If you died tonight, would you go to heaven?" are insensitive, and potentially even insulting.

Years ago, I was working with a gap-year ministry training programme. One term we were focusing on personal evangelism, and the students were encouraged to try sharing their faith with others, and then to report back on how it went and what they learned. One of my students was, like me, a procrastinator. They had been asked to try sharing with someone within a week of the last discussion, and Steven had left it to the last minute. On the morning before the next discussion, Steven realized he had not yet made any efforts to witness to anyone. In his panic to get the assignment done, he asked me to go into the streets with him, so I obliged. Steven stopped the first person he saw, who happened to be a young man from a Far East Asian country. This gentleman's first language was not English, and there would be some huge cultural differences as well. That wasn't going to stop Steven. He went right in: "If you died tonight, and God asked you, 'Why should I let you into my heaven?' what would you say?" The Asian man looked confused. With a puzzled expression, he simply asked, "What?" Steven repeated the question: "If you died tonight, and God asked you, 'Why should I let you into my heaven?' what would you say?" Needless to say, poor Steven didn't get anywhere at all in his conversation with the Asian university student. I hope Steven learned something, and was able to critically reflect on where things went wrong. I know that not all direct witnessing efforts go as badly as this one did, but it does illustrate the point. I am not arguing that these methods should never be used. What I am saying is that if you are going to use them, do it thoughtfully and prayerfully, and most importantly, they should not be the only evangelistic efforts your youth ministry employs.

We Don't

Let's be really honest here. Some of us just don't do evangelism at all. This is either because we haven't figured out the best way to share Jesus with young people, taking into consideration safeguarding, ethics, and the effort it takes, or perhaps it's because we've committed to caring for and discipling the young people we already have. Or perhaps we think there's just not enough time to devote to the evangelistic task. Or worse, some just haven't thought about it at all.

This leaves us with an even bigger theological problem. For Christians, the Great Commission is one of the most famous passages in all of the Bible. After his death and resurrection, and just before he ascends to the Father, Jesus says, "All authority in heaven and on earth has been given to me. Therefore go and make disciples of all nations, baptizing them in the name of the Father and of the Son and of the Holy Spirit, and teaching them to obey everything I have commanded you. And surely I am with you always, to the very end of the age" (Matthew 28:18–20). In our efforts to avoid doing something poorly, it is not an option to avoid doing it altogether. The old adage calls this "throwing the baby out with the bath-water". Jesus commanded us to go in his name, teaching others about him, and offering the life-giving power of grace to others. The fact that he says we are to go "baptizing them" is proof that we are to share that message with non-Christians. At the risk of oversimplifying things, let's put it this way: if Jesus commanded it, we have a responsibility to do it!

In addition to the commandment, there is also the issue of the *authority* of Jesus. So often when I hear others talk about the Great Commission, they start with verse 19: "Therefore go." But the quotation from Jesus begins before that. It starts in verse 18 with, "All authority in heaven and on earth has been given to me." On the one hand, this demonstrates the need for obedience as we illustrated above: Jesus has the authority to command us to witness; we have the responsibility to do it. On the other hand, this concept of authority should also give us a bit of comfort, even a sense of security. When Jesus sends us out on mission, we go in his authority. This means we go in his power, in his name, and ultimately what happens is up to him. I can share the love of God without fear of how others will respond, knowing that ultimately it's up to him to bring about conversion. As Paul says in 1 Corinthians 3:6–8, "I planted the seed, Apollos watered it, but God has been making it grow. So neither the one who plants nor the one who waters is anything, but only God, who makes things grow. The one who plants and the one who waters have one purpose, and they will each be rewarded according to their own labour." It really is *his* mission after all – we just get to take part in it!

As such, our identity as Christians is tied to our commitment to mission. After all, the word "Christian" means "Christ-like". It really isn't possible to separate our Christian witness from our Christianity. Being Christian means sharing Jesus with others. I overheard someone once describing evangelicals: "Telling an evangelical not to witness is like telling them not to breathe." I think the sentiment is true for all who have fallen in love with Jesus, no matter the flavour of their Christianity. In short, evangelism is not optional. As youth workers, this includes our approach to youth ministry. If we cannot simply opt out of Good News sharing in our personal life, how can we opt out of it in our Christian work with young people?

A New Way?

In summary, we have discussed a number of different approaches to evangelism in youth ministry. We've identified the four main approaches as events-driven, peer-to-peer, detached, and non-existent. Although events-driven approaches put a lot of effort and funds into creating sharp events to get young people's attention, they miss the mark by primarily making evangelism about an event, thus de-emphasizing the importance of ongoing relationships. Peer-to-peer evangelism rightly emphasizes empowering young people to share Jesus with their friends. However, a downside is that adult youth ministers may not be able to model how to do this, resulting in us getting young people to do our evangelism for us. Detached approaches to evangelism are commendable for their boldness in their commitment to sharing the gospel, but the unpredictable nature of outside environments, as well as the types of personalities needed for such endeavours render them effectively unsuitable for many who undertake youth ministry. Worse yet, if it's done poorly, it can actually have a negative impact on attempts at sharing the gospel.

Beyond all this lies another theological question: do our attempts at evangelism even work? Evangelism is sharing the Good News. How do we know when we've achieved "success"? Is it when some young people finally say "yes" to Jesus? Is that the end of evangelism? If so, how do we reconcile that with Jesus' command to "make disciples"? Jesus spent three years of his life engaged with twelve disciples non-stop (except for sleeping and the odd moment of alone time). This being the case, it seems like saying "yes" to the call to follow Jesus might just be the beginning of the task of evangelism, rather than the end. Let's put it a different way: perhaps it is time to see evangelism and discipleship as two sides of the same coin, rather than separating them into two distinct movements, like so much of the contemporary Church has done.

From the previous chapters, we are beginning to see that a new model for youth ministry is needed. Attractional models of youth ministry are insufficient on a variety of grounds, and other models, while appropriate in some settings, may not work in others. Some have opted not to engage in youth evangelism at all, but this is a radically unfaithful departure from our theological commitments as followers of Jesus. For youth ministries that do engage in evangelism, it seems that we can break them down into two categories. The first is those who engage in sharing faith in sacred spaces: church buildings, youth halls, etc. We might refer to such buildings and spaces as *our space*. Detached youth work and other forms of street evangelism do their gospel work out there – in *their space*. But what if these weren't the only two options? What if there was a way to come together in the middle, in a shared space? A middle ground?

Reflection Section

How does your current youth ministry programme (or one you have been involved with, or observed) do outreach and evangelism? Were you able to identify with one or more of the three approaches covered here?

Which of the identified approaches to youth evangelism does your own current youth ministry employ? Does one apply to your ministry more than the others? If so, why did you choose that one?

What do you think of our critique of that method or approach? How do you feel about our assertion that some significant changes are needed to the current methods of youth evangelism?

Was a method described that you haven't used, but that you might be encouraged to try based on the description of it here? Why or why not?

What are the problems or limitations of doing youth ministry and outreach entirely in church spaces?

Have you found other helpful ways to do youth outreach that crosses the barrier of sacred spaces?

4

What is Middle Space?

It was a chilly night in November, 2008. My family and I had just moved from the United States to the small village of Rudgwick in West Sussex in the south of England. We'd been standing out in the cold, dark field for our first Bonfire Night experience.[19] Having only been in the area for just over a month, we were slowly trying to find ways of meeting young people. As a 30-something-year-old man, this task was more difficult than I'd imagined. The village church only had a handful of teenagers, and I'd been tasked with opening a youth centre within the next year that would be open to all, church background or not.

As we were leaving the field that night, I saw them. Dozens of teenagers huddled in an aggregate mass. The youth worker in me wanted to walk over to them and engage in conversation. The rational side of me talked myself out of it. Anyway, what would I say? And how would they react to me? Would I come across as a weirdo? Pervert? I was stone-cold terrified.

Then it hit me. I don't know if it was the Holy Spirit or just the realization of what I'd got myself into, but the voice was clear: "This is my congregation." As sobering as that thought was, it wasn't any more helpful at determining how to reach out to young people in my area. Where would I even start?

What developed over the next few years was a subtly different, but entirely new way of doing youth work: Christian discipleship-based youth ministry and open access youth clubs run side-by-side, in the same space, always looking for ways to integrate and build bridges. This method evolved organically for us, out of a desire to reach young people ethically. So we first assumed everyone would be doing it, but the more I talked to church youth workers in my area, the more I found that it wasn't a common approach at all. We have already highlighted the most common approaches to evangelism in youth ministry: hosting an evangelistic event, empowering young people to share Jesus with their friends, or, in rarer cases, detached forms of witness. Of course, none of these methods in and of themselves are bad. They simply do not go far enough. Further to the point, if we are honest, some of us also have to admit we simply do not do evangelistic outreach at all.

Over the years, I've found a number of what I call "Middle Space" youth projects popping up all across the country, but it's taken me longer to find them. As we will see in later chapters, one of the biggest strengths of the Middle Space model is that it is adaptable to a number of different local and cultural contexts. I've seen the approach in a city-centre church utilizing music and art spaces. I've also seen it in a suburban context as an indoor skate park/youth ministry. I've also seen it take the form of a community youth centre in a rural village. Although each of these contexts is radically different from one another, the principle of meeting and journeying with young people in a shared space is consistent. So if Middle Space is not simply about the physical space, then what makes these approaches different? The difference lies in the relationships with the young people themselves, and in the way they integrate evangelism and discipleship into a singular whole. Those who practise Middle Space ministry have committed to getting to know young people, and journeying with them in a way similar to what a missionary might do if they moved to another country.

What is Middle Space?

The concept of Middle Space is very simple. It's not *our* space. It's also not *their* space. It's somewhere in the middle – coming together in a shared space or a neutral ground. Most youth ministry – in fact, most ministry efforts by the Church at large – takes place in some sort of sacred space. By this, I simply mean that the things we call youth ministry happen inside church settings. Granted, it may happen in a specially designed or dedicated space within the church building, or on the church property, but nonetheless, there is a strong sense of attachment to the church building. In this regard, youth ministry has just followed the lead of the wider church.

In the general Church, this includes things like evangelistic sermons, Visitors' Sunday, shared meals with an invitational emphasis, special presentations at Christmas and Easter, choir concerts and dramatic performances, etc. A similar approach has been taken in youth ministry.

The salaried youth pastor – or volunteer youth leader(s) – teaches and preaches to primarily churched young people, who are encouraged to invite their friends to youth groups, weekend retreats, and social events. Even those who utilize less traditional outreach methods like hip hop concerts, gaming tournaments, or rock gigs evangelistically are still using means that require church buildings, because these events happen in *our space.*

A smaller percentage of outreach evangelism happens entirely outside church buildings, or in *their space.* This can include wonderfully apostolic efforts like prison ministry, hospital visitation, street evangelism, door-to-door witnessing, and other forms of front-line evangelism and outreach. In most churches, this accounts for a small fraction of a local congregation's evangelism efforts. This type of ministry takes place in youth ministry less often, with a few exceptions. Some youth ministries are known to take semi-regular mission trips, or get involved with homeless ministry or other forms of poverty ministry. We have already mentioned Detached approaches to evangelism so there is no need to retread that ground here.

Middle Space proposes a third way. Rather than asking non-Christians to cross the huge barrier that is the threshold of the church doorway, or assembling teams of believers to go out into the streets or another uncontrolled environment, this model ventures to meet people on middle ground – environments that are neither *our* space, nor *their* space, but instead *middle space.* Those who undertake a Middle Space model do not start by asking, "What programme of ministry can we do here?" Such ministry does not start from a place of action, but from a place of learning, questioning, and dialogue with the local community. It asks, "What are the real needs of the youth?"[20] Or, to rephrase it evangelistically, "Who are we trying to reach? And what will it take to reach them?"

I can hear some critics now retorting, "But isn't this approach centred too much on the young people themselves?" This is something we might call *anthropocentrism*, or being too centred on humanity as opposed to God or the Scriptures. I suppose there is a danger of that, but only if the foundation of the Great Commission is forgotten – that is, the call to go with the authority of Jesus and the power of the Holy Spirit to communicate the Good News. Just as surely as the disciple of Jesus needs to work faithfully to interpret the Holy Scriptures, one must also work to interpret the local culture. Bible scholars and theologians call this practice "exegesis". It is the process of drawing out the meaning of the Scriptures in a way that is faithful to the sacred text. In youth ministry (and other forms of outreach ministry, for that matter), this process of cultural exegesis is just as important. How will we do outreach with young people if we haven't taken time to determine their needs and receptiveness to the gospel?

Taking together these tools of cultural exegesis and contextualization (from chapter 1), the principle of Middle Space can look radically different when utilized in different settings – and although our book is primarily concerned with youth ministry, the Middle Space concept can also be applied to a number of ministry initiatives in the wider Church. In an inner-city environment, it might look like a homeless ministry that cares for the whole person: the stomach is fed, the person is loved and cared for, and the gospel is shared in tangible ways. On a college or university campus, it might look like a discussion group in a café. In a musical or artistic neighbourhood, it might take the form of a music venue or art gallery that doubles as a church plant or Fresh Expression[21] utilizing the same space. In the town or suburban church, the middle space might be a church-sponsored skate park or sports facility where the goal is to build relationships and integrate Christian content in a way that is natural and organic, rather than forced or imposed.

The problem with conventional forms of evangelism is that most of them are Attractional in nature. As such, evangelism tends to happen within the church walls, and thus its target audience is severely limited. To put it more bluntly, Attractional evangelism is largely aimed at the already-convinced, or, as some put it, "seekers". Seekers are those who are not yet Christians, but who are interested. At the very least, they are people who already have some familiarity with, or interest in, or perhaps even some level of investment in Christianity. Although the efforts to reach seekers with the gospel should be applauded, the seeker-sensitive approach to evangelistic witness does not go far enough. Because the standard practice of conventional evangelism consists of events that tend to happen in church buildings, or similar sacred spaces, it is automatically aimed at either those who are already seeking God out of spiritual curiosity, or those who are convinced of the truths of the gospel, but who simply have not yet committed their lives to Christ.

Middle Space ministry efforts are not aimed only at turning seekers into believers (although it may include that), but also at turning sceptics into seekers. Middle Space youth ministry, then, commits to journeying alongside and supporting young people, wherever they may find themselves on the faith spectrum, even where they have no specific interest in Christianity whatsoever. The Christian youth worker in this context seeks to simultaneously make disciples of those who are following Christ, and also point the way to Christ for those young people who have no interest in the faith. As we stated above, young people deserve our relational support regardless of where they stand on the Christian faith. This is a key difference from most Christian youth work.

Values of Middle Space

Have you ever taken a slightly wrong turn off of the motorway? You approach one of those complicated junctions. You know the type: five to six exits, all looping around one another. It's hard to tell which one is the one you want. You know you need to turn west, but three of the five exits go in a westerly direction and you can't figure out which one it is. Slightly panicked, you have to make a quick decision. Unsure which exit to take, you settle on the second one. Seeing that you're headed due west, you relax a little. It's not until ten miles down the road that you realize it should have been the third exit and you're more than half an hour off course and late for your meeting. "If only I'd paid more attention to the directions!" you think to yourself. "If only I'd asked the right questions!"

Much of contemporary ministry is about asking the right questions. Too often though, ministry practice is guided by the wrong questions. Following the lead of the general Church, youth ministry is no different. We begin by asking questions like:

- How can we get more young people to our church, our youth ministry, our event, or our programme?
- What big event can we put on to reach young people?
- What ministry can we do here in this city, town, or local area?

And just like how a computer will only answer the question we ask it, we only get answers to the questions we are asking.

But these are the wrong questions. Sure, the end goal is noble. What we really want is for more young people to accept Jesus. And that's always a good thing. But these questions lead us to the wrong exit off the interchange. Remember my story about the Xbox tournament from chapter 2? That idea began with a couple of well-meaning questions, such as, "What are teenagers really into?" and, "What event can we put on for them and advertise to the whole community, in order to reach out to more youths?" Well-meaning as they may have been, they were still the wrong questions. I don't know about you, but I didn't sign up to youth ministry to become an events planner. I chose youth ministry because I wanted to make a difference in the lives of young people.

To make sure we are taking the right exit from the motorway, I propose a different set of questions altogether:

- Whom are we trying to reach?
- What will it take to reach them?
- What are the needs of the youth in our area?
- What is God already doing in the lives of young people around us?
- How can we join him?

Attractional youth ministry and Middle Space youth work both have the same goal in mind. Both want to see young people exposed to the gospel with the hope that more of them will come to faith in Jesus. But because Attractional youth models start with the wrong questions, they get the wrong answers. Attractional youth ministry is inevitably numbers-driven. "How can we get more young people to our church?" As such, it is also necessarily events-driven. "What big event can we put on to get more young people here?" Because it is Attractional in nature (attracting young people to our event), it is narrowly focused on "sacred spaces" or church buildings and spaces.

Do young people come to Jesus in these environments? Of course they do, and we are certainly not trying to take anything away from that. But a youth ministry that is driven by numbers, and driven by events, necessarily falls short of the ideals of the kingdom of God. I know that's a hefty statement, and I'll need to qualify it. The reason I think that youth ministry that prioritizes numbers over people and events over needs falls short, is because it emphasizes quantity at the expense of quality. I am not arguing that numbers are bad, or that large youth ministries are wrong. I am simply claiming that we should prioritize the right things.

Middle Space youth work, while also having the end goal of young people coming to faith, has a different starting point and a different emphasis. By design, Middle Space youth work is about people, rather than numbers. It's about journeying with young people, rather than about flashy events. It's about shared spaces, not sacred spaces. Rather than trying to coerce young people into our ministry event, those who practise Middle Space ministry are instead journeying with young people in such a way as to *offer* the gospel. Instead of asking, "How can we get *them* (i.e. young people) to accept Jesus?" we ask, "How can *we* (i.e. the faith community) offer the Good News of Jesus?" This assumes we might be offering it to those who are not yet ready to receive it, and that's OK. Remember, it's about journeying with young people. Instead of asking, "How can we get kids into our sacred spaces?" perhaps we could ask, "How can we meet with young people in a shared space?"

So once again we ask, what exactly is Middle Space? Simply stated, Middle Space is a ministry model in which Christian discipleship and outreach/evangelism are deliberately intertwined, where youth ministry happens neither in *our space* (church buildings or other sacred spaces), nor in *their space* (their homes, hangouts, in the streets, etc.). It happens in a Middle Space. However, it is much more than that. We will examine the model through the following five elements of Middle Space ministry: *location, heart, posture, goal,* and *theology.*

We have touched on the idea of *location* already. Middle Space most often utilizes so-called "third spaces" (not our space, not their space, but a third space), but it does not necessarily do so. It is possible to recreate sacred spaces in such a way as to make them into a Middle Space through creativity, activities or services offered, and finding ways of bringing people together – specifically those who already follow Jesus and those who do not.

Theoretically, Middle Space might be achieved by an *event* held in a church building. As paradoxical as that might sound, it's true. We've railed against events-driven ministry in sacred spaces, so how could I make such a claim? Remember, Middle Space is as much about the concept as it is about the physical space. Are there events, conversations, or programmes that your youth ministry could initiate that would be designed to create a middle ground, building bridges for dialogue and journeying together? Hot Chocolate Trust is a Christian youth charity based at Steeple Church in the city centre of Dundee, Scotland. Because they find themselves in a downtown, urban environment, they do not have access to separate buildings or spare land. Nonetheless, they've found innovative ways to create Middle Space environments within the church building itself, including spaces for a sports room, music room, art room, chill room, etc. (We'll look at their model more closely in chapter 11.)

Let's be very clear though. Middle Space youth ministry assumes the utilization of some sort of dedicated space, given to work with young people. It is not enough to simply rope off a corner of the church sanctuary and put a sign up that says, "youth group". In order to create the concept of Middle Space – a true coming together of mind and heart – there must be a middle ground in time and space. Although there are exceptions (as noted above), this most often happens in a building or facility dedicated for the sole purpose of youth work. There are practical reasons for this type of dedicated space: not having to share space with other groups (a toddler group, knitting club, or choir practice) means not having to set up and tear down for each session, thus saving a lot of time and effort. However, there are much deeper reasons for this, too. A dedicated space, used solely for youth work, allows the young people to take ownership of the space and feel a deep sense of connectedness to it and to each other. There is something very powerful about young people walking into a facility and knowing – as well as feeling – that it is just for them and their enjoyment.

The *heart* of Middle Space ministry is one of bridge-building. Simply doing youth work in a third space does not make it Middle Space, as unfortunately, it is possible to change locations but still do the same things. In the United Kingdom, where I currently serve in youth ministry, from time to time I'll have a conversation with someone about Middle Space ministry and they'll reply, "Oh – you mean third spaces!" But I'm very resistant to this language. If all we do is change the location of our events-driven youth work to a separate building away from the church, we have not gone far enough. Sure, the change in location might take one step in lowering the threshold people have to cross to get into the church, but it's not really a significant change in methodology, only location.

Bridge-building involves getting people who know and follow Jesus to interact in meaningful ways with those who have not yet committed themselves to the Christian faith. This might mean gathering around a common cause with shared values (for instance, a mutually beneficial recycling project). Or it might mean intentionally gathering Christians and non-Christians alike together around a game or fun activity. What makes these efforts distinctly Middle Space is the level of intentionality that goes into them. We deliberately build bridges that make it easier for others to cross over and get a better view of what faith in Jesus looks like. We want to be clear here that we do not simply mean building a bridge to the mainstream church.[22] Unless there's a one-way sign up, bridges allow for traffic both ways. Our assumption here is that it is just as appropriate for us to learn from young people as it is for them to learn from us. The end goal of Middle Space youth ministry is not simply "more bums in pews". Simply getting more young people into the church building, or even into church services, is an insufficient goal.

The *posture* of Middle Space is that of a student, not an expert. The first thing any Middle Space practitioner must do is to learn. The new youth worker moves into the area and first learns all they can about it. What does the micro-culture look like? What are the sights, sounds, and smells of the neighbourhood? What are the needs, hopes, joys, and fears of the area? This will inevitably mean trying some ideas that do not work. That is a perfectly acceptable way to learn. An expert, however, is incapable of learning. Start by assuming you know very little about what it would be like to minister or do outreach in the city, town, or village. This will give you a great vantage point from which to go on a shared journey with those with whom you hope to share Jesus.

I was once at an event where Gavin Calver was speaking. This was a marquee full of youth ministers at a large Christian festival. Gavin boldly asked the crowd, "Let's see the hands of everyone who is failing in youth ministry!" Only a few brave hands went up. He quipped back, "The rest of you are not trying enough new things." I had to admit he had a valid point.

The *goal* of Middle Space is faithful serving. It is with the end hope of evangelism – sharing the Good News about Jesus. This does not necessarily mean converting large numbers of people to Christianity. Whereas most evangelism tactics are aimed at turning seekers into believers, proponents of Middle Space are just as content to turn sceptics into seekers. We find it rewarding to serve faithfully, even if we don't see the masses coming to faith in Jesus – but not because we don't want that to happen! On the contrary, we are content with serving faithfully *because* we know that so many people do not know the hope and joy found in serving the Lord Jesus, and there is much work to be done! Rather than simply starting Attractional youth programmes, Middle Space practitioners will be actively seeking to find out what local needs exist, and ways they can help address them.

Taking the wrong exit from the motorway – even one that heads in a similar direction – will not get us to the correct destination. That is, of course, not without a lot of backtracking, re-routing, and making up for lost time. In much the same way, a youth ministry that is driven by asking the wrong questions will inevitably lead to finding the wrong answers. The final defining element of Middle Space is its underpinning *theology*, which we will delve into in the next chapter.

Reflection Section

What is the starting point for Middle Space youth work? What about the end goal? Why are these important?

What are some of the "wrong questions" that have traditionally been asked in youth ministry? Which of these have you asked in your own work with young people?

What is the essence of Middle Space ministry, in your own words?

What are the five elements of Middle Space youth work? Summarize the first four (we haven't explored *theology* yet) in one to two sentences each.

5

Theological Foundations of Middle Space

Having considered the values of Middle Space youth work, as well as an overview of the first four elements of it, it's time to consider more fully the theology of Middle Space ministry. We'll look at this through a fivefold lens: incarnational, apostolic, postmodern, multigenerational, and organic. But first, I need to tell you a bit more about my own story.

Our call to do missionary youth work in England was very clear. So how then does one go about doing youth work in this new setting, considering a few very distinct obstacles? First, we are in a new country, an unfamiliar environment with differing cultural backgrounds. One can be forgiven for thinking English and American culture are virtually the same, given the shared language (well, sort of – my English friends love to playfully point out how American English is a different language!). Yet, there are a number of key differences in American and British culture and society, including a distinct historical perspective and a differing religious context.

A further, and more personal, obstacle became clear not long after we arrived in England. Having received a call from God to do youth work with a missional-evangelistic thrust, we encountered the very practical and logistical problem that I was in my mid-thirties and didn't know any young people, other than a small handful of youth from church families. How does one go about doing community youth work in a new country, having come from a disparate cultural background, and not knowing many teens?

The answer is simple, but not easy: I had to assume that almost everything I thought I knew about youth ministry no longer applied, except the most basic of principles: prayer, time, relationship, presence, the Word, etc. In short, I had to become a student. Our early days were spent in prayer, in having conversations with locals, listening to parents, meeting teenagers slowly – and, I must add, appropriately.[23] We did not begin by starting new ministries – how would that even work if we did not know the needs of the local community! Rather, we began by serving, and by helping out in things that were already taking place. This was aided by the fact that the building we were to use for our youth centre was under renovation and would not be ready for another four to five months. I used the time to get to know the local area, helped out as a parent in the local school, and got involved in the local Scout group.

What became clear, and may seem obvious to the reader, is that by starting slowly, by listening and learning, our approach to youth ministry in the rural south of England was able to evolve organically and naturally. In fact, if our success or longevity doing youth work in this village could be attributed to any one factor, it would be our posture from the beginning as learners. If ever I am asked for advice or input into youth ministry, I answer with this very thing: go as a student, not as a saviour.

The Attractional models of youth ministry seemed out of place in rural England. Facets of these models are in place in the United Kingdom, and in urban or suburban environments they may work as well as they do in the United States. Of course, we are arguing that even in those contexts, there are shortcomings, or even worse – theological problems – to Attractional models of ministry. Aside from that, Attractional models of youth work simply are not appropriate in rural villages. By and large, people do not drive from one village to the next, or to the larger town down the road to attend church. At least locally, there is more of a sense of connectedness to one's own community. Instead of trying to attract a large regional following of young people, it became more appropriate to try to build bridges locally instead. So the question became not, "How can we build this youth ministry and attract more young people to our programme?" but rather, "How can we begin discipling the young people already connected to the church, and simultaneously reach out to young people in our village who have no faith?"

A foundational assumption of my theology of ministry is that a faithful, healthy, functional church is a beautiful and wonderful thing. Some readers may then pose the question: why the need for a new approach to ministry? If the church is such a great thing, why not just enter a traditional pastoral ministry and focus on doing church really well? This is, of course, a very good question that has merit on its own. The person who is called to ministry, and has a burden for sharing the love of God with those outside the church, would be justified in taking on a role as a lead pastor or senior church leader, equipping the church to serve and compelling others to take on the evangelistic calling, given to us by Jesus himself. As we've seen already, it is very clear from the Great Commission in Matthew 28.18–20 that we disciples are to go in the authority of Jesus, to proclaim the Good News, and to make more disciples.

So the question then becomes, why Middle Space youth ministry? In my own life, my commitment to a Middle Space approach to outreach came about as I encountered, participated in, and subsequently rejected Attractional approaches to youth ministry. I came to see a need for a new approach to evangelism that did not rely too heavily on the need for people to enter a church building, particularly those who were unlikely to do so based on their unfamiliarity with the church or even their complete lack of exposure to it. Similarly, I also found Attractional models of outreach rely too heavily on event-based and numbers-oriented evangelism.

The Fivefold Theological Lens of Middle Space

Middle Space Ministry is Incarnational

There is a lot of talk in youth ministry circles about being incarnational. Although the term is not without its criticisms, it is not our place to get into a detailed theological analysis here. What we mean here by "incarnational ministry" is simply ministry that is modelled after the sending of Jesus – the God in flesh – to be with humanity, even becoming a human, in order to save us. On this basis, Middle Space youth work is incarnational in its approach. It is not merely a "come and see" gospel, nor only a "go and tell" gospel, but both.[24] Kenda Creasy Dean, reflecting on the sacraments, describes incarnational ministry beautifully: "God actually enters the world through human beings, decisively in the Incarnation but also in flawed human practices like baptism and the Eucharist, pilgrimage and prayer – practices God chooses to indwell and employ to give us missional imaginations, and transform us into followers of Jesus."[25] Although Dean's reflections here may describe God's presence in the sacraments, she also, perhaps inadvertently, describes what is meant by incarnational ministry. God comes down in the form of human flesh to make "his dwelling among us" (John 1:14). Taking our cues from Jesus, we go out in the power of the Spirit, to dwell among those who are – like we once were – far from God.

Middle Space youth work that is intentionally incarnational takes seriously the accusation that Jesus was "the friend of sinners" (Luke 7:34). When my children were much younger (primary school age), my son's friend once said, "Your dad is friends with lots of naughty teenagers." I had to admit he was right. Although it might have been confusing for his seven-year-old mind to comprehend, I actually took his statement as a huge compliment. By taking an incarnational approach, a commitment to be with young people, we are content to be salt and light, day in and day out, saturating our words and actions with prayer, asking for the presence of the Holy Spirit at all times, whether teaching a Bible study or playing a game of soccer. Whereas Attractional youth ministry sees evangelism as an event that we put on, incarnational youth ministry sees evangelism as a lifestyle that we live out day to day. Following the pattern of Jesus himself, Middle Space practitioners seek to be incarnational. As Jesus left his rightful place in heaven to come down to earth and be with us, we too leave our ivory towers and fancy church buildings to journey with young people, who otherwise might not come into contact with Christians.

Middle Space Youth Ministry is Apostolic

In addition to, or perhaps by virtue of, it being incarnational in nature, Middle Space youth ministry is also apostolic. By this we mean it takes seriously the issue of being sent by Jesus to bear witness to him (the Great Commission in Matthew 28). We take seriously the *missio dei* (the mission of God), or as Dean puts it, "God's sending of God's own self into the world in human form".[26] As I have stated above, our call to youth work in England was a call to mission. My role here is an integrated role of youth work and missions work. We have not moved to the exotic jungles of an undeveloped country, but nonetheless, the Lord called us to cross-cultural ministry in another country with different cultural customs.

However, there's something even more striking here: youth work is *always* missionary work. Dean clarifies, "Adults in youth ministry have long viewed themselves as missionaries to an alien culture, a special breed of anthropologists who must learn the language, taboos, artifacts, and rituals of the teenage universe in order to make the gospel accessible to them."[27] Christian youth work is a missionary enterprise because it necessarily involves translation. I probably don't have to tell anyone reading this book how adults and young people often speak a different cultural language. Youth ministry includes the work of translating the Good News of the gospel into the language of a culture that is not our own – specifically, the culture of the young people in our area (wherever that may be). The Middle Space youth work model embodies the missionary spirit in that it is attempting to build bridges to the Church, or to the faith, that otherwise might not exist. By Church here we obviously mean the entire church universal, not any specific building.

We will discuss this more below, in terms of how this plays out practically, but it is worth mentioning here some goals of Middle Space bridge-building. One very helpful objective is simply getting Christian young people and non-Christian young people interacting in healthy and meaningful ways. Similarly, Middle Space allows for introducing non-Christian young people to adult Christians, which helps those with little exposure to Christianity to see that we are "normal people". All jokes about what is "normal" aside, a clear obstacle to outsiders embracing the faith is the myriad of misconceptions they might have about what it actually means to be Christian, so attempts to gently remove such obstacles can be helpful tools in bridge-building. Though Middle Space most often does not happen in sacred spaces, it is still beneficial for participants to know they are taking part in church-run initiatives, thus forming positive connections to the local church. Finally, and perhaps most explicitly, an immensely valuable bridge-building objective involves getting young people to take part in sessions where issues of faith are examined more closely by means of prayer, worship, Bible study, and reflection.

Middle Space youth ministry is also apostolic – or a missionary enterprise – insomuch that it is an effort at planting a church. As we alluded to earlier, our own journey towards Middle Space youth work began with a desire to plant a church (that is, to start a brand new church). This was fuelled by a desire to bear witness among those who were not yet followers of Jesus, and it eventually led us to leave our previous Attractional youth ministry role. When we first accepted the call to do youth ministry in England, it seemed either that this call was a sidestep to our desires for church planting, or perhaps that we had misheard that call to plant in the first place. I have since come to believe that neither is the case, but that Middle Space youth work holds the potential for planting a form of church. It is no coincidence that our desire for church planting well over a decade ago was to plant a church that didn't look like most of the churches we were already familiar with. We wanted to target outsiders, not just disenfranchised churchgoers. We entertained the idea of meeting outside of traditional church structures and buildings. We wanted to use music and the arts as media through which to communicate the gospel and share experiences.

Looking back, it is difficult to determine how much of our "call" to church planting originated in God's sending us, and how much of it was led by our own desire to do something different. Of course, there is also the possibility that it was a bit of both! Nonetheless, a few observations about Middle Space youth work are relevant here. If youth ministry is making disciples of young people, isn't that planting a church? If that youth ministry is inviting young people who don't know Jesus across the bridge, and helping them to connect to a living faith in the resurrected Lord, aren't they planting a church? Although we have recognized above that a youth church cannot in and of itself be all the church is intended to be (I contend that by definition the church must be inter-generational), a youth ministry that is truly making disciples and doing evangelistic outreach is contributing to planting and/or growing the church.

Finally, Middle Space youth work is apostolic in nature because it takes the priesthood of all believers seriously (1 Peter 2:9). Youth ministers, in a way, take on a priestly role as they seek to shepherd or pastor young people. By this, I do not mean that youth work requires ordination or ministerial credentials. Rather, all who belong to Christ are sent by him to take his message to others. If this type of youth ministry is to succeed, it must be the project of the local church, or perhaps a few churches in a region coming together. Although one person may lead it, one person cannot make it happen on his or her own. It must be a team project. It is important, then, to involve faithful Christians who are able to pray effectively (James 5:16), and who are also "prepared to give an answer to everyone who asks [them] to give the reason for the hope that [they] have" (1 Peter 3:15).

Middle Space Youth Work Is Postmodern

We have stated above that our shift from Attractional youth ministry models was, in part, inspired by a desire to do evangelism differently. We have acknowledged the problem of not being around non-Christians enough when so much time was spent within the church walls. We have also mentioned that Middle Space youth ministry, being intentionally incarnational, is focused on neither "come and see" models of evangelism, nor "go and tell" exclusively, but strategically utilizes both. Furthermore, Middle Space evangelism does not centre around events – though events may be utilized – but centres around lifestyle, including both words and actions. Middle Space youth ministry can also be decidedly postmodern in its approach to evangelism.

The term postmodernism describes a massive cultural and philosophical shift that developed in the mid to late twentieth century. It is characterized by scepticism of the intellectual assumptions of the previous era, the Modern era. The Enlightenment and Renaissance periods ushered in a huge sweep of scientific discovery and technological progress. The downside of this was a certain commitment to certainty, leaving little room for mystery. The postmodern era sees shifts towards tribalism amidst increasing globalization; towards scepticism in an era when it seemed that science could answer *everything*; and towards relativism in the face of moral clarity. As a result, many churches either rallied against science, making it a spiritual enemy, or on the other hand looked to prove tenets of the faith in a scientific-rational sort of way. Although there is too much history and philosophy to delve deeply into here, there are some observations worth making about youth ministry in the postmodern era.

In sharp contrast to the black-and-white certainty of the modern era, youth evangelism in a Middle Space context is narrative-based. Stories are generally more compelling than arguments. Christian young people, who are being made into disciples of Jesus, live out their testimony and share it when given the chance. These young people are taught the importance of testimony and are given the chance to practise articulating their faith in discipleship sessions which take place in the same physical space as bridge-building outreach sessions. Although apologetics may be helpful in understanding the ins and outs of one's faith, or in forming rational thought processes, testimonial itself is not argumentative, but narrative. Testimony sides with the blind man who was healed. When asked if Jesus was a sinner, in lieu of presenting a debate or argument as a response, he exclaimed, "Whether he is a sinner or not, I don't know. One thing I do know. I was blind but now I see!" (John 9:25).

A narrative approach to evangelism is rooted in love rather than anxiety. Instead of asking, "How many kids have committed to the faith?" we ask, "Who are the kids we've befriended?"[28] Such an approach is more ethical as well. Much youth evangelism tends to be fear-driven, based on exaggerated stories, or fear of consequences. This includes doubling down on the fear of hell, or lives wrecked by drugs and alcohol or promiscuity. We are not saying these things are not real issues that occasionally need attention, or even a stern warning. But on the contrary, narrative evangelism is love-driven, content to journey with young people, share stories and testimonies, and trust the Holy Spirit. It is based on the love of God rather than the fear of hell.

The second way that a Middle Space approach to youth evangelism is postmodern, and more ethical, is that it is not based on selling an idea. Just as one's testimony is not argumentative in nature, it is also not down to emotional manipulation. Rather, the gospel-oriented way of life offers the Good News freely. The Good News of the kingdom has come down in the person of Jesus, and we walk in the way of that kingdom. "Come and join us!" we cry. To borrow an economic term, the gospel is put out into the "marketplace of ideas" amongst other competing world views, but is offered freely and without manipulation or coercion. This becomes incredibly important, considering the concept of Middle Space. The goal is bridge-building, with relationships built on trust. Parents who have no faith allow and even encourage their young people to take part in the activities and services offered. Those of us who offer such activities must take that trust seriously and be good stewards of it. Our Good News must really be good, and not simply emotional manipulation in the guise of "preaching the gospel".

Middle Space Ministry is Multigenerational

A Middle Space approach to youth evangelism is also multigenerational. Adults model narrative, ethical, conversational evangelism, and young people who are on the journey of following Jesus exemplify peer-to-peer evangelism. As they have practised telling their stories, they are also able to share them with their non-Christian friends. Bridge-building also takes place in an invitational spirit as they invite their friends to discipleship sessions, or to take part in weekend camps or adventure breaks. In fact, peer-to-peer invitation is key to Middle Space youth work. This is distinct from a mode of youth ministry in which the salaried youth worker is expected to have all the answers and carry all of the vision. We are also not talking about exclusively peer-based evangelism, which we critiqued in chapter 3. Peer evangelism is essential both as a means of sharing the gospel and for growth and development of those who are already following Jesus as they step out in faith and boldness to tell others about God's love. Peer evangelism is only problematic when it is the only method of evangelism employed in a youth ministry.

Although they were not writing about anything resembling a Middle Space approach, Ashton and Moon in their classic work described the merits of multigenerational ministry: "Young people need to discover faith in a concrete way, and the most concrete way is in the life of another young person whom they know well. Adult models of faith are important, but the most immediate impact will be the faith of another young person or, better still, the faith of a group of young people. We therefore need to be setting up opportunities for a positive Christian peer group to be established, so that the faith can be modelled from Christian young people to one another and to their non-Christian peers."[29] Families are invited to take part as well, as we offer a listening ear, or prayer for family needs or struggles.

Aside from the theological reasoning, there are practical reasons for a multigenerational approach. Although it is often assumed that younger adults are more suited for youth work, that is not always the case. Older folks can often come across as non-threatening, grandparental figures. An obstacle I have found in my own youth work is that I myself am a parent of teenagers. Many of the members of my youth group(s) are peers to my own children. Although this is not in and of itself a bad thing, it does create a particular challenge for confidentiality. Do these young people see me as the youth worker they can talk to about important and/or personal issues, or do they see me primarily as their friend's dad? Older volunteers at our youth centre do not have the same obstacle. I have found that many of my best and most dependable volunteers are retired folks – perhaps they have more free time to give to such work!

Middle Space is Organic

The starting point of Middle Space, as we discussed in the last chapter, is asking the right questions. This allows us to take the right exit off the motorway and continue on the right track! Being people-driven and not numbers-driven, exegeting (interpreting) the local culture, and looking at the needs of young people in our area – all of these allow us to grow organically and naturally. Attractional youth ministry is events-driven and asks the wrong questions. The only way to follow up with a successful evangelistic event is to put on a bigger and/or better event next time. The way of Middle Space is different. Events are planned in response to a specific need, or as a healthy and organic way to continue to build relationships.

Rudgwick, the rural village in England where we worked until recently, has a small outdoor skate park. As the village youth worker, I helped raise some of the funds to build the park. I also helped manage it: liaised with the young people who used it, helped report any issues or repairs that needed to be made, etc. After the skate park had been open for a few years, there was a small, tight-knit group of young people regularly using the park. One of them was keen on photography and used to set up his camera and take videos and still shots. The level of skill at the park at that time was quite high. How could we bless and encourage those young people in the skills they were developing? At their suggestion, we decided to host a competition, known locally as a "Skate Jam". Although we were utilizing an *event* to do youth work, it was happening organically and naturally – and, it is worth highlighting, at the suggestion of the young people themselves! We held three such Skate Jams in three consecutive years, and then that particular event fell by the wayside. There was no point in forcing it to become an ongoing annual event when that was clearly no longer the need. Nonetheless, we would readily have taken up the cause again if there had been significant interest.

The point is organic growth. In our open youth club sessions, we had access to a large playing field. We didn't own the field or have exclusive rights to it, but the youth centre sat right on the edge of the field. Additionally, behind the centre was a strip of woodland. Our location on the field, as well as the rural nature of our group, led us to play a lot of outdoor games. We regularly played soccer, rugby, Frisbee games, and a whole host of "wide games". Wide games are simply outdoor games played over a wide range of space: things like Capture the Flag, Virus, Manhunt, and a slew of others. These games would be unlikely to work in urban or even suburban environments, but they were a natural extension of our work in rural West Sussex.

Although we are talking about an organic approach to the kinds of events and activities we put on, there is a larger point here. Too much of contemporary ministry involves forced types of "growth" (I'm hesitant to even call it growth, hence the quotation marks). Churches often simply copy what other churches are doing. The mindset seems to be, "it worked over there, so it will work here." The starting point of Middle Space is asking the right questions, and we must also continue to ask the right questions as we go on in ministry. The growth of the ministry into new areas, new programmes, and new ventures must always take an organic path – a sort of natural evolution, if you will. From the moment we opened our youth centre in 2008, I described it as "a work in progress". However, it is still, and will forever be, a work in progress. In youth ministry, may we never think to ourselves, "We have arrived." Instead, may we always be open to changing and evolving naturally and organically!

Reflection Section

How would you feel if someone addressed you as "(Your Name), the friend of sinners"? Is that a claim someone could make about you?

In this chapter, we claimed that youth ministry is a missionary enterprise. Do you agree with this? Why or why not?

How much of a role does narrative or testimony play in your youth ministry? Are there ways it could or should be increased?

Do you agree that youth ministry, where possible, should be multigenerational? Why or why not?

Describe the importance of an organic approach to youth ministry. How does this apply to events, growth, and evolution over time?

6

From Sacred Space to Middle Space

One of the crucial issues of youth ministry is the question of location: where does youth ministry happen? As we discussed in chapter 4, a large majority of Christian youth work takes place *at church*. That is, in some type of sacred space. Our physical locations can be either our biggest asset in ministry, or the biggest hindrance to it. Ironically, it is often both, because the building itself shapes the kind of work that is done.

Church, and church

The megachurch where I used to work had a full-size basketball gym, half a dozen small rooms used for Sunday school classes, a larger meeting room for youth group meetings and worship gatherings, and a medium-sized room for a casual hangout space or breakout groups. A portion of our readers can relate to this kind of space, whereas many others are wishing they only had a fraction of that. But bear in mind, even the best church facilities – however you may define what is meant by "best" – are still functioning out of an Attractional mindset. "Build a great facility and people will come," to paraphrase our character from *Field of Dreams*. Although we might observe that excellent facilities attract people to come to them, this mindset ignores a whole host of other problems, both practical and theological.

Practically speaking, this mentality ignores the amount of competition that exists out there in the general marketplace. Young people attend schools where they have gymnasiums and other recreation facilities and equipment. They live in neighbourhoods where there are parks, gyms, swimming pools, and a host of other activities. That's not to mention the music venues, coffee houses, skate parks, shopping malls, and so much more. Simply providing yet *another* facility for recreation will not be enough to attract (there's that word again) young people to want to be a part of your youth ministry. One thing I encourage youth workers to ask themselves is: what is the one thing young people can get at your youth ministry that they can't get anywhere else? The answer to that question may vary – community, a sense of belonging, Christian teaching, identity, and world view – but it will certainly lead us to think about how much effort and finance we put into buildings and facilities alone.

More crucially, there is a theological problem with over-emphasizing buildings, which has to do with the nature of church itself. If you're reading this book, I probably don't need to remind you of the biblical definition of church, but it's worth spending some time reflecting on it anyway. The New Testament word for church is *ekklesia* (ek-lay-SEE-uh), meaning "the called-out ones". It comes from the root words, *kaleo* ("to call") and *ek* ("out of"). As you probably know, theologically speaking, "church" has very little to do with buildings or sacred spaces and everything to do with people. In some ways, it's a shame that the English word for "church" means both the people and the building. I wish that somehow historically we'd come up with a different word for the building than for the body of believers, as this problem has wreaked havoc on what it means to be and do church for over a millennium; I suppose we can blame Emperor Constantine for that. To try to differentiate between the two uses of the word, I will refer to the body of Christ as "the Church" (capital "C") and a local church building as "church" (lowercase "c"). When referring to a local congregation, I will also use "church", to differentiate it from the universal body of Christ or, as the Apostles' Creed puts it, "the Holy Catholic Church".

The earliest Christians met in a variety of locations to worship, pray, and exhort one another in the Word: in the synagogues (Acts 9:20, 13:5, 17:2, not to mention Jesus' own practice of preaching and teaching in the synagogues), in homes (Acts 5:42, Romans 16:3–5), in Solomon's Colonnade (Acts 5:12), in the temple courts (Acts 5:42), and we can assume a variety of other settings. None of these were purpose-built structures resembling what we today call churches. This is not to say that church buildings are necessarily bad. I am only making the point that the place of worship and teaching didn't seem to be of utmost importance. In fact, it wasn't until the fourth century, under the reign of Emperor Constantine, that churches began to be built in a widespread fashion.[30]

Even in the Old Testament, where we get the tradition of elaborate temples for worship, there was a deep tension regarding sacred spaces. Following the exodus, the church in the wilderness was a nomadic people, living in tents. Even the place of worship was temporary. These people were following the cloud by day and fire by night – everything was mobile. A few centuries later, it is King David's desire to build a permanent house of worship to the Lord. Although this noble desire came from a pure place in David's heart – he was living in a palace while the Ark of the Covenant was in a tent – God spoke something entirely different from Nathan the prophet:

> "This is what the LORD says: Are you the one to build me a house to dwell in? I have not dwelt in a house from the day I brought the Israelites up out of Egypt to this day. I have been moving from place to place with a tent as my dwelling. Wherever I have moved with all the Israelites, did I ever say to any of their rulers whom I commanded to shepherd my people Israel, 'Why have you not built me a house of cedar?'"
> **(2 Samuel 7:5b–7)**

The Lord goes on to reveal that David will not build a temple, but rather his son Solomon will. But the Lord's statement above is very revealing – he does not need a human building in which to dwell. Temples of worship are more about our own needs than they are about his. They can serve a beautiful purpose, but God does not need them to do his work!

As I write this, we are living through a unique phenomenon for anyone currently alive. Due to the coronavirus pandemic, we are not allowed to attend or hold worship services in any church buildings. The United Kingdom is in its second nationwide lockdown to try to slow the spread of the coronavirus. Other nations of the world are facing similar situations. If not full lockdowns, then restrictions on numbers, social distancing, face coverings, and a whole host of things we weren't thinking about a year ago have all become commonplace. Hopefully, by the time you're reading this, things have changed and gotten back to a certain level of "normality". We never want to downplay the seriousness of the illness, nor the lives lost because of it, yet it has provided a wonderful opportunity for us to rethink all sorts of things: healthcare, social gatherings, sports, live music, education, and – yes of course

– church and youth work! Let's be honest, we've needed to rethink the last two for decades, even centuries. Many of our most insightful writers and thinkers have been imploring us to get back to a New Testament understanding of church as *ekklesia* for quite a long time. Covid 19 forced us to do just that.

Sacred Space and Middle Space

Much more than a physical location, Middle Space is a concept. It is an approach that is not content to assume people will come to us looking for salvation. After all, most people who are not Christians are not even aware they need saving. In this approach, we are also not content to spend the majority of our efforts out on the margins – at least not without inviting those on the margins in for a cup of tea! Our theological commitment is to the truth that the Church ultimately is the body of Christ, made up of people, rather than a building made of bricks, mortar, and wood. As long as the crucial elements of Church are present (worship, prayer, fellowship, the Word, sacrament), then Church can take place anywhere. Although the concept of "sacred space" is deeply ingrained in humanity, my assumption is that it is not the physical location that makes the space sacred as much as what happens in those spaces.

Having said that, it is important to note that by definition, Middle Space youth work requires a physical location. It is distinct from both Attractional youth work ("our space") and also Detached youth work ("their space"), and instead invites Christian and non-Christian alike to come together on a neutral ground. Middle Space takes place in a *shared space*. An important aspect of youth work in any setting is that the young people themselves should be able to take ownership of the youth ministry. The best practices in youth work will allow young people to take part in decisions, in the ministry itself,[31] and in owning the space.

Well over a decade ago, an important piece of research was undertaken in the United Kingdom. Sally Nash, Sylvia Collins-Mayo, and Bob Mayo conducted an in-depth five-year research project among youth in the UK, mostly among young people who did not have a Christian or church-based background. In regard to the importance of space they found, "One of the attractions for the young people was that the [youth] club provided youth oriented space. This is unusual compared with the other places young people routinely occupy; various scholars have noted that young people have very little creative autonomous space, either in the public or private sphere."[32]

It is this middle ground between the youth's autonomy, and adult guidance and supervision, that turns the physical space into a place. "Place can be thought of as meaningful space – a physical location filled with significance, history and identity."[33] Even in Attractional youth work models, ownership of the space by young people is important. The thoughtful youth worker, lead pastor, or church architect – or in the best scenarios, all three working together – will design the space with the young people in mind, rather than simply giving them what is left over. Better yet, the young people's voices, as well as their needs, will help guide the process of designing the space. Similarly, in Middle Space youth work, having a dedicated space is essential. More often than not, these spaces are found or created outside the church: a community youth centre, a sports or music hall in the middle of the city, or an outdoor space in a rural area that is repurposed for meaningful connection, among others. In chapter 11, we'll look at specific examples of Middle Space approaches and the types of spaces they are utilizing for youth work.

A word of caution at this point: Middle Space youth work that is not done in a traditionally held sacred space (i.e. in a church building), but rather done in a neutral, dedicated youth club, faces the danger of making the youth club a Place—a meaningful space—instead of the church. The implied danger is that young people learn to value the youth club as a place of belonging rather than the Church. In response to this, we must remember a few things. First, Middle Space youth work emphasizes sharing the Good News of Jesus with young people through word and deed, regardless of the location, thus de-emphasizing the sacredness of any physical location. The Church is people, the body of Christ, not a building. So there is no real danger of young people becoming emotionally or spiritually attached to the youth club over against attachment to the church building.

Additionally, Middle Space youth work is about building bridges to the faith of the Church, meaning at some point non-Christian young people may be invited by their Christian peers into another sacred space, i.e. a church, or to a Christian camp or overnight residential retreat. More importantly, as the processes of disciple-making are taken seriously, young people all across the spectrum of faith and background will be encouraged to remain connected to the Church – the body of worshipping believers – beyond their involvement in the youth ministry.

Third, if we take seriously the concept of the Church gathered, then the Church is present in the youth club as we gather to sing, pray, share testimonies, have fellowship, and study the Scriptures together. The church building is no more sacred than the youth club, as long as the people of God – of any age – are gathered together in his name. Although a Christian youth group in and of itself cannot be the Church (just as an all-white, English-speaking congregation does not represent the totality of the Church universal), it can truly be a faithful representation of the body of Christ, and thus function as a church.

It is worth considering some final thoughts about space and place, namely that the sense of atmosphere and place created in a dedicated youth facility can serve as a form of evangelism in and of itself. This can happen in a rather surprising way: the rules of the club. Most youth clubs or youth ministries run in a Middle Space mindset will have a certain number of rules, most of which will revolve around respecting one another or respecting the space itself. *The Faith of Generation Y* highlights the role of the "youth club as a moral community".[34] The loss of a Christian world view in a post-Christian society will inevitably result, to a certain degree, in the loss of a Christian moral or ethical framework. Although morality can come from a number of different sources, both religious and non-religious, the loss of the particularly Christian moral framework is a real one, but one that Christian youth clubs can help to recover.

Christian youth clubs – both explicitly religious ones and those with an open youth club approach – can help young people develop moral and ethical thinking by providing opportunities to discuss issues of morality, right and wrong, etc. Nash et al. found that both churchgoing teens and non-churchgoing young people had recognized the important role that youth clubs had played in helping to develop their thinking. They continue: "Another important influence on young people's learning about right and wrong came from the rules of the club. Obviously there were times when unacceptable behaviour in the club was corrected. But more than this: the young people themselves recognized the value of the club's rules and took ownership of them themselves... By imbibing the club rules in this way the young people implicitly took on something of the Christian culture, although they were not necessarily aware of doing so."[35]

Of course, taking on something from the Christian culture cannot be equated with receiving the Good News of Jesus and committing one's life to it, but it is certainly a step in the right direction. When combined with deliberate and intentional bridge-building and cross-pollination with more explicitly Christian discipleship opportunities, the possibilities become even more promising. Some of this is down to the deliberate and intentional creation of atmosphere. Of course, we don't simply mean building design, but something much more.

Creating Middle Space: Physical Space, Design, and Atmosphere

I love old, ugly, dilapidated buildings. Perhaps it's my inner punk rocker and the hours I've spent going to gigs in reclaimed spaces, or maybe it's something else. I've always loved the idea of taking an old space – something not fit for human habitation – and repurposing it. In part, it speaks as a metaphor for new life in Christ. OK, that might be a stretch, but hear me out: Jesus takes our old selves and cleans them up by his Spirit to be a place where God dwells. When I was studying in university, at some point I had the idea to open up my own record store and/or music venue, but with Christian purposes. No, not a Christian bookstore with safe, sanitized products and sanctified trinkets. A proper record store as a missional outpost! In those days I used to drive around noticing any old warehouses, rundown office buildings, and other empty spaces. I dreamed of turning one of them into a reclaimed, repurposed space that would serve as a community for doing outreach together through music and the arts. Although that never happened (I could never quite figure out how to fund it, nor how to sell my crazy idea to people who could help get it started), the idea served to plant the seeds for Middle Space.

Few of us attempting Middle Space youth work will have access to large budgets, allowing us to build a new, purpose-built facility. We can, nonetheless, with God's help create an atmosphere that combines the best use of the physical space, a youth-friendly approach to design and décor, and a welcoming atmosphere. Space is not inherently sacred, but physical space is generally necessary (with a few exceptions we'll explore later). Where can you achieve Middle Space both physically and conceptually?

Physical Space

So you want to do Middle Space youth work. You want to reach out to the young people in your community on neutral ground, and also do discipleship. One thing to begin asking yourself, and to begin praying about: what kind of space is already available? You might spend time driving or walking through your community, asking God to provide something. You might also strike up the courage to ask for help. Who are the people in your faith community or your local area who are the "movers and shakers" who can help, or at least point you in the right direction? In the gap-year ministry programme I mentioned earlier, the church we worked with decided to turn the basement level of the church building into a café. A few blocks away lived the Georgia Institute of Technology, a major university set within Midtown Atlanta. Streetlight Café was birthed out of a desire to reach Georgia Tech students in a non-threatening environment. Friday or Saturday nights hosted live music and free coffee (or donations). Although I didn't know it at the time, it was an early attempt at a Middle Space outreach! Even though the café was held inside a church structure, it had a separate entrance, and it looked and felt like a café/music venue. It was a genuine attempt to meet people on a middle ground.

In my current context, I got really lucky. No, actually, the Lord was in it. There was an old, dilapidated cricket pavilion sitting empty. Well, sort of. At the time discussions started, there had been a squatter living in the building to get out of the cold (don't worry, he's in a much better place now and is no longer homeless). In fact, even calling it a "pavilion" is a bit of a stretch. It was a small, brick and cinder-block building, with minimal facilities attached to it.

A new sports facility had been built a few hundred meters away, meaning the cricket club had a brand new home, leaving the old club-house empty. At one point the plan was simply to demolish the building. It certainly wasn't fit for much else considering the state it was in at that time! However, for a number of reasons, they decided to leave the building standing while they deliberated about what to do with it. Enter Rudgwick Church. Although our local village church had done youth work for many years, they'd never had adequate space in which to do it. Consequently, they'd also had part-time youth workers. It was during a local parish council meeting when one member of the council (who was also a churchgoer) brought up the idea of the church using it for a youth centre. Remarkably, the local council members (a secular authority) were delighted by the idea. Their only stipulation was that the club be open to all young people, not just those who were affiliated with the church – something we were eager to do anyway! By the time I arrived in 2008, renovation work on the building had already started. I'm often amazed at the vision, foresight, and dedication to youth work found in this rural parish church. The cost of bringing the building up to code was shared between the church and the parish council. What's more: while the council retained ownership of the building, they agreed to lease it to the church on what's known colloquially as a "peppercorn rent". What this means is that the cost of rent for an entire year is a single peppercorn, "if demanded". It's an incredible partnership that has continued for more than a decade.

Rudgwick Youth Centre is simply one story. In chapter 11, I'm going to tell you about a whole host of churches and other organizations in the UK (and one in the United States) who are employing Middle Space ministry approaches. Each of them has a different story, and I'm confident that each of them will inspire you to think outside the box and come up with creative solutions. I hope my own testimony about our run-down cricket pavilion helps you to see what is possible when you commit to doing outreach and discipleship with young people, all in the same space!

Design

Of course, having a building is only part of the battle. Once you have a space you can use, what are you going to do with it? How are you going to use it? What kinds of things need to go inside? Our small youth club is filled with sofas, a pool table, foosball table, indoor basketball machine, tables and chairs, board games, art supplies, music equipment, and loads of games supplies. The key is not so much what you choose to fill the building with, but the fact that the facility must look like a space for young people! As soon as you walk into our youth centre, you know exactly what it is. There's nothing else the space could be used for, and we're fortunate that we don't have to share it as a multi-use space. You don't have a dedicated space to use? Don't worry, we'll look at multi-use spaces and creative use of space later in chapter 10. Our main point here is that the design and décor of the building must absolutely look like it was designed for youth. Many of us will have done youth work in churches where there was no dedicated space for youth. I've run youth sessions in the choir room, the church fellowship hall, and other non-specific spaces. Although we youth workers are grateful for any space in which to engage with young people about relationships and spirituality, the problem is that in non-dedicated spaces, there is no ownership of the space. The young people know at least subconsciously that the space isn't theirs. If we're not careful, we can be inadvertently communicating that children and young people don't *really* matter – that they're more of an afterthought.

So in a true Middle Space context, intentional thought has to be put into the building itself, the creative use of space, and also how the space is decorated. Legacy XS is a church-run indoor skate park in Essex, just east of London. This suburban church has taken the incredibly innovative position of building a high-quality, state-of-the-art indoor skate facility, and using it as their principal way of doing youth work. We'll talk a little more about Legacy later on when we look at specific examples of Middle Space, but I want to mention something relevant here regarding their use of décor. It is fairly obvious that a skate park does not resemble a church, or a sacred space, in just about any way. Yet, this ministry wants to reflect its Christian heritage in some way, so in addition to the ministry sessions they run there, they have also made use of sacred art to decorate the facility. In the café/lounge area, there are paintings and photographs with sacred designs. Inside the skate park itself, there is a huge sculpture made out of some sort of fibrous, woody material, representing an artistic take on the cross. Although none of these symbols themselves constitute evangelism in the proper sense, they do allow something sacred to penetrate subtly into the consciousness of those who observe them. If nothing else, they constitute a statement of the centre's Christian aegis.

Atmosphere

In addition to the facility (the building itself) and how we decorate it (the design), the third essential element of creating a Middle Space environment involves the abstract yet tangible aspect of atmosphere. An important role of the Middle Space youth worker is creating just the right atmosphere. The coolest renovated building in the world, along with the hippest décor – these alone will not create a place of belonging and ownership. At the risk of sounding Attractional, these alone will not mean young people want to be there. The attitudes of the key leaders and volunteers will add so much to the atmosphere of the place. It is important from the outset of the project to intentionally create an atmosphere of welcome, acceptance, inclusion, curiosity, and fun! We don't talk about fun enough in theological reflection, but in youth work it's essential. If young people don't enjoy themselves, they are unlikely to participate. In my own youth work, I unapologetically state that fun is a core value!

Even though some of the ideals of atmosphere are abstract and difficult to measure, they can nonetheless be cultivated, nurtured, and therefore demonstrated. Most of us will be familiar with the phrase, "I know it when I see it." However, the phrase was coined in less than glamorous circumstances. In 1964, US Supreme Court Justice Potter Stewart was presiding over a legal case in which the banning of a film deemed to be "obscene", that is, containing pornography, was under consideration. In the famous ruling, Judge Stewart failed to define what was meant by pornography, but added, "I know it when I see it."[36] If you'll forgive the crude analogy, *welcome* is precisely like that. I can't tell you precisely what welcome is, but I know it when I see it. I also know it when I don't see it. Think for a minute of a time when you felt like you stood out. Perhaps it was when you were a teen yourself. Or maybe it was turning up to a party when you were clearly underdressed (or overdressed).

When I was a student in graduate school, I was looking for a local church to take part in while I studied. I had high hopes for a little church I visited. I was hopeful for a few reasons: I knew a couple of guys who attended there. The pastor was, or had been, a theology professor at a nearby Christian university, so there was great potential for intelligent preaching. But more importantly, the church was on the "wrong side of the tracks". I was hopeful that this church, set in a rougher, poorer neighbourhood, might reflect something of the kingdom of God in a special way, as churches in those areas often do. When I arrived, no one greeted me. No one said hello. When I sat on the pew, no one sat near me, nor even looked at me. When the service was over, they all spoke to each other, but not to me. As I was literally on the way out the door, the pastor's wife half-smiled and said, "Come back." I didn't say it, but my immediate thought was, "Come back to what?" I never went back.

Perhaps you can relate to my story – via a bad experience at church or as a customer in a shop or restaurant. Fortunately, in my example, I was already a Christian. But suppose I'd come in off the streets looking for answers? Suppose I was really low and desperately needed God's love? Creating the right atmosphere in Middle Space largely boils down to welcome. Young people should immediately be made to feel as welcome as humanly possible – without going overboard, of course. Do you know their names? Do you encourage your volunteers to learn them as well? When a young person doesn't seem to be engaging with anyone, what do you do to draw them in? Don't assume they will be able to sort it out on their own; you may only get one shot to let them feel welcome and accepted! In chapter 8 we'll look more intently at recruiting, training, and keeping volunteers, but every adult on the premises needs to receive training in how to create and maintain a sense of welcome.

Those first few minutes are crucial. Anecdotally, it's been noted that someone will decide within the first few seconds of arrival whether they will attend again. But the atmosphere is about so much more than just welcoming them. What kind of atmosphere are you creating through the sessions and activities themselves? We've talked about Middle Space in regard to the physical space, as well as the concept of meeting young people in a neutral environment. However, there is also a Middle Space in regard to relationships and power. Almost everywhere young people go – school, church, home, in public – adults are in a position of power. Middle Space can create a unique environment: one in which adults and young people are on an equal footing in regard to power. Can young people have a say in what activities are planned or what games are played? Can young people help direct or guide the kinds of faith discussions that take place?

In addition to creating symbiotic relationships, there is a practical element to letting young people have a voice in the types of studies that happen – it helps ensure that we are not simply answering questions that no one is asking. At least once every two years (and sometimes more often than that), we host a sort of "Open Mic" session at the youth club, where for three to four weeks we leave the whole teaching session open to questions young people have. I warn you, it can get messy. Someone might ask something inappropriate. Even more likely is that some clever young teenager will ask a question that I don't have an answer for. But there's something more important than answers taking place. We are caring enough about them to have a few weeks dedicated to the issues that are near to their hearts. Sometimes I have to answer honestly, "I don't know. Let me get back to you." Or even better, "Let's find out together."

Levelling the field of power can also be modelled in our own personal relationships with the young people. Do we model fair play with them in the games and activities, or is it simply about winning? One of my nicknames, bequeathed upon me by the young people, is "Big Kid". I have come by this name honestly, as I tend to get involved in every game and activity we run at the youth centre. I don't do well watching from the sidelines, as it were. However, in playing the games with them, I (hopefully) get to model honesty, fair play, and respect. Mutual respect is a huge part of what it means to be Middle Space. Can you treat young people with the same amount of respect you would want from them? This might be as simple as shaking their hand and introducing yourself when you meet them, trying to recall their name later, or phoning them up to ask how they are doing (especially if you're aware of a particular challenge or grief they are facing). But above and beyond the specific expressions, it's a matter of seeing them as just as important and/or valuable as you see yourself or any other adult.

Wrapping Up

In this chapter we've looked at what we really mean by sacred spaces, what it means to be church, and why Middle Space is needed. We've attempted to describe what Middle Space actually is, and how it can be achieved, by looking at the physical space, the design, and the atmosphere. We concluded by looking at the importance of welcome, mutual respect, and levelling the playing field in regards to power. In the next chapter we'll look more closely at the fusion of evangelism and discipleship, and what that actually looks like in a Middle Space context.

Reflection Section

In what ways has your own facility or ministry space helped in your work with young people? In what ways has it been a hindrance?

How do you feel about the challenge, and also the prospects, of finding (or renovating) and using a Middle Space facility?

What does the word "church" mean to you? Put it in your own words.

In what ways has your experience of church and your definition of church (from above) been affected by either the church as a *building* or the Church as *people*?

How could your work with young people (or a youth ministry you are involved with) improve its practice around the ideas of welcome and atmosphere? What are its strengths and weaknesses in this area?

7

Discipleship in Middle Space

So far we've looked extensively at the Middle Space model, having critiqued – or rejected altogether – other models of youth ministry. We've looked at the different ways various youth ministries approach evangelism and broken them down into a few different approaches. Furthermore, we've looked at the need for a new approach. What does a distinctly Middle Space approach to evangelism look like? And what about discipleship? How can we make disciples if so much of our time is spent doing outreach?

Two Sides of the Same Coin

A teacher once asked her class, "Which wing of the airplane is more important: the right wing or the left wing?" Some of the students looked at her with a puzzled gaze, while a few others chuckled at the ridiculousness of the question. We all know the answer: both wings are equally important. A plane with only one wing would never get off the ground. And yet, how often do we miss the ridiculousness of this analogy when we ask similar questions about evangelism and discipleship? Or worse, we fail to ask the question at all, thereby falling into the rut of doing only one of these to the exclusion of the other?

Evangelism and discipleship are two sides of the same coin. It's worth unpacking this cliché a bit, as I fear it has become so familiar that it's lost its meaning. Take out a coin and have a look at it. Nearly every coin has a "heads" side and a "tails" side – two different images on the opposite faces of the coin. Nonetheless, it remains the same coin. The two sides are inseparable, eternally fused to one another. A one-sided coin does not exist. The same could be said for evangelism and discipleship. The contemporary Church in the Western world has often made a mess of this. We've separated evangelism from discipleship in rather unhelpful ways. We've made evangelism (sharing the Good News) into something that is only done *to* people, specifically non-Christians. And we've boiled down discipleship to something that is done only with *real* Christians, or *serious* Christians. Furthermore, we've reduced both of these things to what happens at events (as we described in chapter 3). We've managed to separate a unity with two elements that should be eternally fused to one another, and we've unhelpfully turned them into formulas and programmes, rather than the natural, organic processes of a living organism.

Contrary to the popular notion that discipleship is something that happens only for the serious follower of Jesus, if we read the Gospels carefully, discipleship starts any time someone encounters Jesus. It's worth pausing here and looking at Jesus' calling of the Twelve to follow him. It may be time-consuming, but an in-depth read-through of all of the gospel passages that deal with Jesus calling his followers will be quite revealing. Jot down your own notes as you reflect upon each of the readings from Matthew, Mark, Luke, and John. So go ahead. Put down this book and grab your Bible. The passages are Matthew 4:18–22, Matthew 10:1–4, Mark 1:14–20, Mark 2:13–17, Mark 3:13–19, Luke 5:1–11, Luke 5:27–32, Luke 6:12–16, Luke 9:1–6, and John 1:35–51.

* * *

One of the things we notice when doing an in-depth study like this is there really isn't a "one-size-fits-all" approach that we can pinpoint in our gospel readings. Some of the early followers of Jesus were fishermen (Simon Peter, Andrew, James, and John). Although the Gospels don't give us the full story, it appears as if these men followed Jesus immediately after meeting him. One minute they're fishing. The next minute they're leaving all their expensive equipment behind and following this Jesus fellow. Matthew (aka Levi) on the other hand is a tax collector. As such, he would have been hated by his fellow Jews. He was a traitor to the Jewish people because he made his living collecting taxes for the evil Roman empire. Jesus calls him to follow him too.

Others of the disciples we know very little about, except that a few of them probably were disciples of John the Baptist before they followed Jesus. This in itself is very telling. We know that John the Baptist's role was to "prepare the way for the Lord" (Mark 1:3). It appears that at least one of the ways he did this was by preaching a message of repentance, or turning from sins, and that the "kingdom of God has come near"

(Mark 1:15). According to John's Gospel (different John, by the way), it seems probable that at least Andrew, Simon Peter, Philip, and Nathanael were already listening to John the Baptist's message when they met the one they believed to be the Messiah. Incredibly, Philip tells Nathanael, "We have found the one Moses wrote about in the Law, and about whom the prophets also wrote – Jesus of Nazareth, the son of Joseph" (John 1:45). For these men, their discovery of the Good News about Jesus, and their call to be his disciples, happened simultaneously! Discipleship, for them, was not something that happened as they got more serious about following the Lord, several years after becoming Christian. It started immediately when they first believed the Good News about Jesus.

On the other hand, as we continue reading the Gospels, we are very often left with the impression that even those closest to Jesus didn't fully understand what he was about. Peter is not only one of the twelve apostles, but also a member of the so-called inner ring of the three core disciples, which also included James and John. And yet after three years of following Jesus, Peter tries to rebuke the Lord for claiming he will be put to death (Matthew 16:22; Mark 8:32). I don't want to tread on shaky theological ground here, but Peter's complete lack of understanding as to what Jesus was all about (as well as James and John at other times), followed by Jesus' harsh rebuke of Peter, makes me wonder: at what point were the disciples "saved"? Was it when they first started following Jesus? Was it after Peter proclaimed, "You are the Messiah, the Son of the living God" (Matthew 16:16)? Bear in mind this proclamation came right before Jesus says to him, "Get behind me, Satan!" (Matthew 16:23). Judas's plight further confuses the matter. He too had followed Jesus for three years. Even knowing that Judas was planning to betray him, Jesus washed his feet, offering him a sign of forgiveness. Moments later he is betraying his master for a mere thirty pieces of silver!

The point is simply this: discipleship is messy. It's up and down, backwards and forwards. We make huge strides of progress, only to be set back by failure, doubt, or sin. The line between the saved and the unsaved isn't always as clear as we'd like to make it out to be. Don't get me wrong, I believe in justification by faith, the security of my own salvation, and yours. It's just not always clear where you and I are in our journey of discipleship. Philip's belief in the Messiah started his discipleship journey immediately. Judas might not ever have started his. I hope we meet him in heaven one day, but we simply don't know.

Let's not forget that Jesus called many others to follow him as well. The most famous of all Bible passages is probably John 3:16, often referred to as the golden text of the Bible. Jesus says, "For God so loved the world that he gave his one and only son, that whoever believes in him shall not perish but have eternal life." This statement about eternal life comes from a private conversation Jesus had with a man called Nicodemus. Nicodemus was a very important man. He was a Pharisee, a teacher of the Jewish law. As you probably know, the Pharisees were some of Jesus' harshest critics. Yet, Nicodemus was curious about what Jesus had to say. It's no coincidence that he came to see Jesus at night, in secrecy. During this long conversation about the new birth and a new kind of spiritual life, we receive this golden text, these very revealing and eternal words about the nature of salvation. Yet, we have no idea if Nicodemus ever became a follower of Jesus or not. Again, I'd like to think we'll see Nicodemus in heaven, but we just don't know.

What about the rich young ruler? He was a young man who was in love with his wealth and possessions. He truly believed in Jesus and wanted to follow him, but when Jesus asked him to give away everything he had, he simply could not do it. He loved his money more than the prospect of following the Messiah. There are countless others: the man who wanted to say goodbye to his family first, or the one who first wanted to go and bury his father. Were they simply making excuses for not following Jesus, or is there more to the story? Again, we simply don't know the rest of the story.

Evangelistic efforts in the Western world are often too simplistic. We overuse tools like the Four Spiritual Laws, the Sinner's Prayer, altar calls, "every head bowed and every eye closed", and related tactics. I'm not against any one of these, per se, but our overuse of them has led our evangelistic efforts to become stale and formulaic. Which of the twelve disciples gave intellectual assent to the Four Spiritual Laws before they packed up to follow Jesus? Bear in mind, the crucifixion and resurrection hadn't even taken place yet! However, these men were already living in "eternal life" with Jesus, having found the Messiah that Moses and the Prophets wrote about! How often did Jesus get his listeners to pray the Sinner's Prayer when he preached to the crowds? (Hint: he didn't.) Jesus invited people to follow him, and to find eternal life if they did.

Even still, that looked different for almost everyone. Some followed him because they ate from the miraculously multiplied bread and fish.

The Samaritan woman believed because she had met a prophet who was able to reveal to her deep secrets about her personal life. Nathanael too followed Jesus because he was astonished that Jesus knew intimate details about his life. In his case, it was his religious devotion. The rich young ruler was asked to give away all of his possessions *before* following Jesus. However, the man from Gadara, from whom Jesus had driven out a legion of demons, desperately wanted to follow Jesus but instead was instructed to stay at home and tell everyone what the Lord had done for him. It appears that the best way for this man to "follow Jesus" was by staying at home. By making evangelism too formulaic, we miss out on the specifics of discipleship. By making discipleship something that only happens after someone has been a Christian for a long while, we make the Good News something that is no longer good, because so few can attain it. By separating evangelism from discipleship, our two-sided coin loses its value and the right-wing or left-wing plane crashes to the ground.

Salt of the Earth

One of the most common conversations I have with regard to spiritual matters in my British context has to do with being *religious*. It comes up in a number of different ways. I'll be talking to a friend about church, or about our faith-based session at the youth centre, and they'll respond, "Oh, I'm not religious." It's a polite way of saying, "I'm not interested." On the other hand, quite often I've been asked by young people something to this effect: "I hear you're really religious. Is that true?" This is, by far, one of my favourite questions to receive. I never answer it outright. If I say, "Yes I am," then I've answered the question and the conversation's over. Never mind the oft-debated topic of whether Christianity is a religion or not, which we won't go into here. More often than not, I like to answer the question with a question of my own: "What do you mean by 'religious'?" This is an attempt to model my conversations after Jesus himself, who often looked beyond the question to something deeper. Think of how often we see Jesus being asked a question, and rather than giving a straight answer, he returns the query with a question of his own! On a more practical note, it carries on the conversation longer, and gets us talking more around what words like religion, faith, spirituality, the Bible, and Christianity even mean in the first place.

You've probably heard the old adage, "You can lead a horse to water but you can't make him drink." Someone wisely once told me, "No, but you can make him thirsty. How do you make a horse thirsty? You give him salt." I find this cliché really helpful for understanding what evangelism looks like in a postmodern, post-Christian world. By claiming we can't force a horse to drink, we are saying that you can offer someone Christianity but you can't force it upon them. This is absolutely true! So the question then becomes, "How can we make others *desire* what we are trying to give them?" In Matthew 5:13 Jesus says, "You are the salt of the earth. But if the salt loses its saltiness, how can it be made salty again? It is no longer good for anything, except to be thrown out and trampled underfoot." Evangelism in a postmodern, post-Christian context does not start by preaching a message to others. In fact, it doesn't even start with a message. It starts with us. We start not by asking, "How can I get others to believe what I believe?" but rather, "How can I make my own life and beliefs fall more in line with Jesus Christ? How can I be more like him?" We read in the Gospels how the crowds followed Jesus. Sure, they wanted to see the miracles. They wanted the loaves and fishes, the healings. But many of them also wanted his words. In essence, they wanted *him*.

Middle Space evangelism takes all of this into account. Evangelism doesn't happen as the result of a big, flashy, Attractional event. It happens day in and day out. It is a message that is embodied and lived out by those who have received the Good News and its life-giving joy for themselves. It's worth doing some soul-searching here, both individually and corporately, and asking, "Do we have what it is we're trying to give away?" A true Middle Space approach keeps evangelism and discipleship fused together, as we invite young people who are already following Jesus, and those who are not yet following Jesus, and even those who do not believe in a God at all, to come together in a shared space, a neutral ground.

Middle Space Discipleship

If Attractional evangelism is events-based, then it follows that discipleship will be programme-based. Discipleship in these contexts will involve systematized programmes and structures, organized like rungs in a ladder. Of course, there is nothing wrong with a good programme of ministry. However, purely programmatic ministry efforts will inevitably become formulaic rather than organic. Just as the call for the disciples to follow Jesus took different forms, so does continuing to walk with Jesus. In contrast to the Attractional model, discipleship in Middle Space is built on relationships rather than formulas. It is based on people, rather than programmes.

We've already discussed the concept of Middle Space as it regards the physical space used for youth ministry (it's not our space, nor their space, but somewhere in the middle). We've touched on how it relates to relationships of power (it's not our power, nor theirs, but a coming together in a new form of equality – sharing ideas together). There is also a meeting in the middle in regards to discipleship. Although this is facilitated by the shared space, it extends much deeper to the ethos of the ministry. In a standard, Attractional, church-based model of youth ministry, evangelism and discipleship are separated, in a rather unhelpful manner. Discipleship takes place only for the already converted. Ironically, often evangelism takes place that way as well. How many young people have you met that "got saved" every year at summer camp? Both evangelism and discipleship are aimed at young people already within the sphere of church influence: either those who are already committed to the Christian message and lifestyle, or at least those who are already convinced of its validity.

In a Middle Space youth ministry, evangelism and discipleship are fused together, and they happen in the same space, often outside of the church walls. In our rural context in England, this looks like a local, community youth centre. Everyone knows that the youth club is run by the church. They also know that the youth club is for everyone, regardless of faith, belief, or background – or the lack thereof. There are a number of distinct sessions throughout the week. Some are for teaching and discussion in the Christian faith: Bible studies and discussions, prayer and worship, leadership training, etc. Many of these sessions wouldn't look too different from a standard Christian youth group, but the space in which these take place allows outsiders to take part more easily. This same space is also used for "open youth clubs". An open youth club is a session for young people that is not specifically religious in nature. Such sessions will take different shapes depending on what kind of facility is used, the local context of the club, as well as who is running them. They are designed to get young people together, having fun, getting to know one another, and – especially – building trust and relationships with the youth worker and the team running the club.

We could look at these sessions as "earning the right to share the gospel". There is a tricky line to walk here. We warned in an earlier chapter about the unethical nature of bait-and-switch tactics. So we are not here talking about introducing a sneaky "God slot" into the open youth club sessions. Our primary concerns here are building relationships of trust, and supporting young people regardless of where they are on the faith spectrum. Nonetheless, some intentional and strategic cross-pollination can occur here. It is likely that Christian young people will attend both the faith-based sessions as well as the open youth club sessions. Young people who are comfortable in the setting will be more likely to invite their friends along to a faith-based session, or even to a Christian camp or retreat in due course. Likewise, young people who do not identify as religious will feel more comfortable attending a discussion group at the youth club where they already attend, than they would attending a church service, simply because they are already familiar with the space and comfortable with the leaders whom they already know and recognize.

We now see that an invitational approach – as long as it is not the *only* approach to evangelism – can function as an important piece of a larger puzzle. Every year in our youth work in Rudgwick (well, not counting 2020, but that is another story altogether), we did a weekend camp in our region, attended by roughly 500 young people. The whole camp was sponsored by the Church of England in our diocese (all the Anglican churches in our two counties) and had a strong Christian theme each year. Most years our group, in addition to many young people from churchgoing families, took along a few young people with little to no church or faith background whatsoever, simply because (a) they already attended an open session at the youth club; and (b) they were invited by one of their Christian friends. We were very clear about what they were signing up for. I usually told them: "It's a Christian camp, and I want you to be aware of that before you sign up. But don't worry; just get involved at whatever level you feel comfortable. We're not going to force you to do or believe anything you don't want to." Both the young people and their non-churchgoing parents seemed to appreciate the honesty.

Taking this approach means we have to be OK with whatever choices the young people make regarding their own faith – or lack of it – in the long term. We always place the relationship with young people as the highest priority, even as we hope and pray that they too will come to know the living God. I've seen young people come to faith in these environments. Some of them have grown in their faith, despite their parents' lack of involvement in Christianity. Others have said "yes" to Jesus at a camp, and haven't appeared to really progress beyond that initial decision. Others have ultimately decided it's not for them. Even in these cases, we are pleased to have had the opportunity to share God's love with them as best we can.

On one such occasion, we had taken a teenage boy with us to the Christian camp. His parents were friends of mine, despite our vastly different religious beliefs (or lack of them). The boy was friends with some of the lads who attended our discipleship group, so he decided to come along, knowing full well what the camp was about. One afternoon, as lunch was being prepared, we were all sitting in our camping chairs inside the meal marquee having Group Time. In the usual manner, we were going around the circle, each saying one thing that had impacted them in some way. This lad stood up and announced proudly, "I'm an atheist!" I don't know if he thought we'd get angry, or what kind of reaction he was expecting. I simply responded, "OK. Are you having fun?" He said, "Yeah, I am!" And that was that. Although some readers might be disappointed I didn't engage him in a full-on debate regarding an apologetic argument for the existence of God, my purpose was much more simple (and hopefully longer lasting) than that. I'd gotten a hardcore atheist kid to attend a Christian camp, enjoy himself, and feel comfortable enough to open up to the group about where he was in regard to spiritual matters. This was a huge win.

Another young man I worked with was an even tougher case. This particular boy had been in a lot of trouble. I got to know Troy after he started attending our open youth club sessions. I came to find out he had been in trouble multiple times with the police, mostly for minor things: vandalism, shoplifting, and other acts of anti-social behaviour. He had been in trouble enough times that he was under a strict curfew – no leaving the house after 9:00 p.m. *unless he was attending the youth club!* That's right – he had special permission from the police to break his curfew if he was at the youth club. He even had a collar on his ankle so they could track his movements. I had built up some trust with Troy and his mother by going along with him on his check-ins with the local police. He had to report to the police station once a week, so on a few occasions I drove him in when his mother couldn't go with him. Over time, he also came to attend a few of our faith-based sessions, and eventually came to our Christian camp. He even went as far as to get prayer at one of the festivals. He seemed to be impacted by the experience. Afterwards, I asked him what he thought about it all. His answer was both refreshing and disappointing: "Oh, I believe in God. I just don't want to start talking to him and stuff like that." Perhaps somewhat like the rich young ruler, he went away without us knowing really what happened to him spiritually. He's an adult now, but I still bump into Troy from time to time. Hopefully one day I'll be able to have another conversation with him about where he is spiritually, and what he thinks about the Lord. To reiterate, Middle Space evangelism and discipleship are messy. They're fused. Sometimes that means they're all a bit mixed up. We have to be OK with that. Our contemporary approaches to evangelism sometimes put "winning souls" before the relationship, pushing someone to make a superficial decision before they are ready to do so.

Then there's Jonathan. He was one of the boys who came to faith through the ministry of the youth centre. Jonathan's grandmother attended church, but neither of his parents did. There was a loose connection to the faith, but no specific commitment. Jonathan started attending the faith-based sessions at the youth centre and took to them immediately. He was the kind of boy that showed leadership potential, so we put him to work. He would run the PowerPoint slides for my talks or help set up the audio equipment. It wasn't long until he showed interest in leading stuff on his own, so I got him doing some things up the front, including some short talks or presentations. At one point he got really interested in the idea of testimonies. He was fascinated by stories of God working in people's lives, and he started collecting these stories and then sharing them with the youth group. As Jonathan and I were discussing the next week's session, I encouraged him to share his own testimony. Like so many teens, he didn't think he had one. He seemed puzzled when I pressed him gently: "When did you become a Christian?" He opened up, "I don't think I have yet." I was blessed to lead Jonathan in a prayer of commitment to Christ. I am delighted to report that Jonathan is still following Jesus to this day. He's studying medicine at university and I'm certain he'll continue to use his gifts and talents wherever he goes.

Jonathan's story illustrates clearly the fused nature of evangelism and discipleship. He'd been attending, taking part in, and even leading in our discipleship sessions long before he ever committed himself to Christ. In other words, he was already being discipled long before he became a Christian. Middle Space allows for, or even thrives on this sort of ambiguity. In summary, Middle Space discipleship is built on the priority of relationships, cross-pollination via the culture of invitation and the empowering of peer evangelism, and it is embodied in the shared space that is inhabited by both the open youth club sessions and the faith-based sessions.

Structuring Discipleship Sessions

So how do we actually do this? What does Middle Space discipleship look like in practice? As any hermeneutics professor will tell you in every situation: "context is key." Your discipleship sessions need to take a lot of things into account, so you'll need to start by asking yourself some key questions. These questions will help you to create an informal group profile before you schedule a single session.

Which young people am I looking to do discipleship with? I would encourage you to put names and faces here. What do you know about these young people? For instance: "Jack, eleven years old, year 7 at Central School. Strong church background in his father's family. Crazy about rugby. Ellen, twelve years old, year 8 at Eastside. Attends Sunday school once a month, and has shown some interest in stories about Jesus. Enjoys musical theatre. Hugh, thirteen years old, year 9 at Central. No church background, but shows a sparkling curiosity in deeper conversations at open youth club sessions." No one will see this except for you and whichever team members are assisting in this process, so feel free to include any relevant or helpful bits of information.

How old are the young people you are working with? Are they younger teens or older? The type of teaching/discussion material you use could vary depending on the answer to this question. Do you have an even spread across the age groups, or are there gaps somewhere? For instance, we went through a challenging phase where we had lots of 16- to 17-year-olds, and a handful of 11- to 12-year-olds, but nothing in between! Structuring our teaching and discussion sessions was incredibly difficult. Eventually, we decided that trying to bridge the gap wasn't working. In the end, we created a brand new session specifically designed for 10- to 13-year-olds.

Similarly, as best you can tell, where are these young people spiritually? Are they already following Jesus and in need of some help and encouragement to do so? Or are they simply curious about the Christian faith and in need of a little more persuasion to look into it more? You might ask it this way: what is the overall "spiritual climate" of the group you hope to disciple? This will include things like having a rough idea of their biblical literacy, how comfortable they are about sharing their own views and opinions, and how much support they receive from parents or other significant adults in their faith development.

These questions need to be addressed before you begin thinking through the more practical issues of running a youth session. After you've established an informal group profile, you can begin doing some further market research.

When should your group meet? That will depend on the needs of the young people and their families, as well as the availability of your team members. When I was a teenager, my youth group always met on a Wednesday evening. That was the general pattern in the denomination I grew up in. So years later when I became a youth pastor, guess what night we had youth group? Wednesday, of course! I didn't even bother to ask the question of whether that was the best time or not. Later we underwent a restructuring of our discipleship ministry and had to revisit this plan. School nights are increasingly busy for many reasons: homework, early bedtimes for younger youth, after-school clubs and sports, etc. So how do you choose a day and time? You need to do some market research. Phone potential members of the group and/or their parents. Tell them about your plans, what you hope to do and achieve. Either you can ask them when a good time would be to host such a group, or you could suggest one: "We've been thinking about running this on a Sunday afternoon, so it doesn't conflict with sports and homework; would that work for you and for Jonny?" Getting parents on board early can go a long way towards solidifying the group. Most families will appreciate being asked for their input early on in the shaping of the session.

In terms of structuring the group itself, an important question is: *how long will a session last?* This will of course be driven by (a) what you are trying to accomplish in the sessions; and (b) the answers to your informal group profile. Will an hour be long enough, or does it need to be an hour-and-a-half? I would strongly discourage anything beyond two hours or anything shorter than one hour, but even these discrepant lengths need to be determined by the kinds of young people you have and what you are hoping to accomplish. Some further questions need consideration here: Where and how will you build in social time, group games, activities, or ice-breakers? Will there be music or some type of worship? Are small groups or discussions built into the session? What about snacks and drinks? Will they be provided, or is there a snack shop in the youth club? All of these considerations will factor into the length of time in the session itself.

Let's get down to the nitty-gritty. *What kind of format will you use for discipleship training?* I want you to think back to your own youth group days (if you attended one). What kind of teaching styles were the most effective in your own spiritual or faith development? Do you remember any of the talks or discussions? If so, what made them impactful? I would encourage you to continue to reflect on that as you think through your own group structure. If you did not attend a Christian youth group growing up, perhaps think about a teacher or coach who made an impression on you. What was it about them or their methods that stand out to you to this day?

Perhaps you are thinking of structuring the youth group like a youth worship service/youth church – a time of worship followed by a talk from one youth leader – perhaps delivered in a sermonic style. Would this format be right for your group? I can't answer that for you. It is certainly one valid way to run a youth group, but it is not the only way. What about using visual slides or something similar? Some educational studies suggest that the use of visuals enhances the learning experience and the ability of young people to absorb information. What about small group discussions or breakout groups? Some youth ministries utilize small groups as their main point of teaching, whereas others use them to expound upon and discuss material that has been delivered previously by a main speaker. Will one leader consistently be the main teacher/speaker, or will you share the load between a handful of youth leaders? Will you allow young people to contribute to the teaching in some way, or to lead a small group?

So, which of these is best? Truth be told, all of them are appropriate. They all work. The task is for you to determine which one is appropriate for your group. I highly encourage you to utilize each of these approaches across your tenure. Different young people gravitate towards different teaching and leading styles. Some young people prefer a sermonic style (it's true, I've met some), whereas others like to engage in discussion. Others are not comfortable, or haven't yet developed the confidence, to share their own thoughts or ideas with others. Generally speaking, I try to change teaching methods for each term or unit of study we go through.

One term/semester, we may look at a book of the Bible together in a small group setting. Each group will have an adult leader (or perhaps an older young person who is confident leading a group). The groups might use a guidebook, or handouts you've prepared. The following term we'll switch things up entirely. It might be a topical study on an issue (for instance, sexuality and the Bible, or a Christian response to the environment), using a series of visual slides. The following term I'll produce handouts and pass out pens/pencils so they can fill in their own answers and write down their own thoughts as we go through. Changing things frequently may be challenging for those of us who don't like change, but it also helps keep us from getting into a rut. Utilizing different teaching methods also helps us to "reach" each young person and connect with them via a learning style that resonates with them. If we only take one approach all of the time, it is likely we are not connecting with at least one-third of the group. Across any given year, a Christian youth worker should attempt to circulate through two to three different formats for teaching and discussing Christian content.

One of the biggest challenges I've faced in our discipleship sessions is finding suitable resources. Finding material that is engaging, theologically responsible, age-appropriate, biblically literate, *and* suited to your doctrinal commitments can be challenging. Many of you will be comfortable and have the time to write and develop your own resources. Others of you will have to spend long hours combing through your Christian bookshop, or online resource shops, to find something appropriate. Others might use denominational materials. Whichever one you choose, always know that every resource you use is adaptable – whether it says so or not. You can add your own game or discussion material, or leave out that extra film clip if you don't have time in your session or because it's not appropriate to your setting. On the flip side, this also means that no resource is "ready to use" straight out of the box, even if it claims to be. You need to do your homework when it comes to reading through the material for yourself and adapting it to your needs: stressing a doctrinal emphasis (or underplaying one), adjusting it to make it more age-appropriate for your group, etc.

Unfortunately, there isn't really a shortcut to the process of finding or creating suitable teaching material. Rest assured, however, that it is time well spent. It is perhaps one of the most important things you do. At the same time, it's OK to relax here. Remember how we asked you earlier to recall a teaching or discussion from your own teenage years? I suspect that many of us cannot remember one clearly. Yet, I'm confident that all of us remember a youth pastor, youth ministry volunteer, or small group leader who invested time and energy into our lives and shaped us in a positive way. The relationships are just as important as the teaching content.

The Role of Adult Helpers in Discipleship

We're going to spend the next chapter looking at how to recruit, train, and utilize adult helpers across the whole of your Middle Space youth work. However, a chapter on discipleship would be remiss if we didn't address the role of other adults in the discipleship process. Having the right team of adults assisting in youth ministry can multiply the impact of your work. Youth ministry is not and cannot be a DIY endeavour. Nowhere is this truer than in attempting to make disciples. Although it can be difficult to find the right helpers, there are a few bare minimums that must be taken into consideration. The first is that volunteers serving in discipleship efforts must have a living faith. Whereas it is appropriate to be inclusive of all young people in the youth ministry, it is essential that the adult staff are all "singing from the same hymn sheet". An adult helper who is sceptical or cynical about the Christian faith may unintentionally do more harm than good. In the next chapter, we'll address appropriate ways to involve people from all across the faith spectrum in Middle Space youth work, but for discipleship purposes, there needs to be a bare minimum of a commitment to the lordship of Jesus Christ. In order to make disciples, we need to first be disciples. This also extends into lifestyle commitments. Although we don't want to be the morality police, make sure you are choosing people who are modelling the kind of lifestyle we are promoting to the young people.

Another aspect to think through when choosing adults for discipleship roles is personality. Here I am probably not going to say what you might expect. So many times I've read job advertisements that want a "charismatic" or "outgoing personality", which I think is all wrong. Are we saying that introverts can't serve in ministry? However, we're also not saying that personality doesn't matter at all. Our minimum requirement here is someone who can be warm and friendly. You don't want someone with a harsh personality who is going to put young people off from coming. If they are at least warm and friendly, then it doesn't matter if they're also shy or outgoing, boisterous or quiet – the youth themselves will be all over this spectrum, so it is appropriate for this diversity to be reflected in our youth helpers as well. However, it does matter that they actually care about youth and generally like people.

We're going to talk more widely about roles in the next chapter, but it's worth thinking about them here in specific regard to discipleship. How can you best utilize other adults in your youth ministry? Are there young persons that would benefit from one-to-one mentoring? Mentors can be helpful for a number of reasons: developing leadership qualities (for instance, pairing up a young guitarist with an adult worship leader for personal growth and development), or as in the case of Troy whom we mentioned earlier. Mentoring a young person who's been in trouble might drastically change their prospects for the future if they're paired with the right person who can help them ask the right questions and move towards a different set of behaviours and outcomes.

A helpful way to look at discipleship roles is to consider what gifts and talents the adult volunteers bring to the table. Are they talented in music, sports, speaking in front of groups, or another area? Are they a bubbly extrovert who would be great at leading a game? Or a quiet but friendly face with a warm smile who would be great at the registration desk? Some people prefer to look at the roles that need to be filled (e.g. worship leader, drummer, sign-in/register, prayer team, small group leaders) and then find people to fill the roles. Others prefer to find the kind of quality people they want and then find or create roles for them to fill. Neither of these are right or wrong, they're just different ways to approach things. When I worked in a larger church setting, I would have adopted the former approach. In smaller settings and rural areas where I haven't had dozens of people lining up to volunteer for youth ministry, I've had to take the latter approach. To be honest, I actually now prefer the latter approach as it puts the emphasis on the people and their gifts as opposed to a role that I think needs to be filled. Taking the former approach can also lead us to get caught in a ministry rut where we have to always do the same thing, meaning we then try to force people into that mould when it might not be a natural fit for them.

When I was a graduate student, I volunteered in a local youth group. I became good friends with the youth pastor, Mike, and he became a sort of informal mentor to me. He took the people-based approach to utilizing youth helpers. Knowing that I was a big music lover, he found ways to bring that out and put me to work in the youth ministry. It also helped that there were a lot of kids in the youth group that were also into music (this was the 1990s after all). In addition to occasionally playing in the youth worship band, Mike had me introducing Christian music to the youth group. Fairly regularly, he would have me do a short "music review" to the young people. I'd play a short snippet from the CD or cassette (anyone remember those?) and then talk about the lyrics and/or why I liked the music. We also started a small music library where kids could check out an album and bring it back the next week. This was not a role that previously existed – it was created because Mike saw my passion for music, and some creative ways that it might benefit the young people and connect with them in a personal way.

Bridge-Building Opportunities

We've considered how the physical space of Middle Space allows for cross-pollination in both evangelism and discipleship. We've also discussed how empowering peer ministry and creating a culture of invitation can contribute to the effectiveness of a fused approach. We can also help this process along through the structure of the ministry and the utilization of purposeful events to this effect. You've probably noticed I used that dreaded word, "events". Let's just address this now. We are not talking about relying on event-based evangelism or programmatic approaches to discipleship. Having railed against Attractional forms of ministry, we are not now going to advocate for them. What we are talking about is a holistic approach to Middle Space: one in which building relationships takes priority, and which can be enhanced by empowering peer evangelism, a culture of invitation, and the utilization of purposeful events. So what do we mean by events that are purposeful?

Purposeful events in Middle Space are bridge-building opportunities. Again, we don't necessarily mean building a bridge to the church

– wherein the goal of youth ministry is increased attendance in a church service (though that may happen). By bridge-building, we mean relationally filling in the gaps between Christian and non Christian, young person and adult, culture to culture. The most obvious way we do this is at open youth club sessions. In my current role, I spend time every week with young people who do not know or follow Jesus Christ. It is one of the most satisfying aspects of my work with teenagers.

There are also several other bridge-building opportunities:

- *Camps, retreats, and residentials*: because of the relationships we have built with young people, we have made it easier for our Christian young people to invite their friends to an overnight Christian camp or retreat. As I mentioned above, every year we have young people with no faith background whatsoever taking part in an intensive Christian camp, with full disclosure about what they are getting themselves into. If nothing else, it's a fun weekend away from their parents and/or siblings!

- *Social activities*: here we mean activities separate from the normal open youth club sessions. These might be special events like laser tag, paintball, bowling, discos, beach trips, and so forth. This is another great way to get churchgoing young people interacting in natural ways with those who do not attend a faith-based session. It's great seeing the surprised looks on the faces of young people, followed by, "You go to youth club?" "Yeah, I go on a Wednesday night [faith-based session]. Which one do you go to?" "Oh, I go on a Tuesday. What do you do on a Wednesday, is that the Christian one?" I have seen this exact conversation, or a reasonable facsimile thereof, play out many times and it's really refreshing to watch.

- *Adventure activities*: these are extended social activities, but they up the ante, adding some sort of physical and/or mental challenge. This includes things like a canoeing trip, a long-distance hike, or a challenging bike ride. They might take place overnight, like a camp, but have a different focus. Some of our events have included a twenty-mile bike ride, a twenty-five-mile hike in the Yorkshire Dales (national park full of small mountains/large hills), and an overnight canoeing trip. A few years ago we hosted such a canoeing trip, with a low-level Christian theme of "I Can", based on Philippians 4:13. Throughout the weekend, the young people were encouraged to work together, while tackling challenges like building a fire with no matches, setting up a tent on dry ground (even though we were in a flood zone), and canoeing down a river that had overflowed its banks due to heavy rain. I'm actually glad the river wasn't as gentle as normal, as my entire goal for the weekend was for them to be challenged at an appropriate level, and encouraging them to think about where they might find help. One young man whom I had never been able to get to attend any other Christian event took part, simply because of the adventurous nature of it.

- *Service projects*: community service projects are another great bridge-building activity in a number of ways. There is the obvious cross-pollination: Christian young people and non-Christian young people working together towards a common purpose. However, engaging young people in a service project is in itself engaging them with an important aspect of Christianity: the importance of serving others. Who knows what is occurring within the young people spiritually as they act out the Christian faith that they have not yet embraced? In our village, we've helped the elderly tidy up their gardens, cut back overgrowth on pavements, and helped clean up neglected areas of the parish.

As always, context is key. Will all of these activities or events be appropriate in your setting? Possibly not. However, it is worth taking some time to brainstorm and chat with your team about creative ways to make the most of bridge-building opportunities, utilizing what would be natural to you and your group. A group based near the sea might host a surfing or coasteering event. A group near a lake might do an overnight fishing trip. Urban groups will likely have different interests to rural groups and vice versa. The key aim here is making the most of the momentum you have built in your open youth sessions and taking it a few steps further.

Reflection Section

As you read through the gospel narratives of Jesus calling his disciples, what stood out to you? What surprised you?

What do you think about the claim of this chapter, that evangelism and discipleship need to be fused together?

In the section on structuring discipleship sessions, we talked about the need for an informal group profile as you decide how to structure your sessions. Begin writing your own profile.

Reflect back on any youth group teaching you may have received as a young person. Which styles or formats did you connect with the most? What was the most memorable talk, discussion, or faith-based youth session you remember? How will this inform the way you plan sessions for the young people you work with?

Plan a brainstorming session with your team. What are some possible areas for cross-pollination and bridge-building? What will you plan this year that will get Christian and non-Christian young people, as well as your youth ministry team, interacting in healthy and natural ways?

8

Youth Ministry is Not DIY

I have never, anywhere, ever, met a youth worker who said to me, "You know what our problem is: we just have *too many volunteers!*" Whether you call them volunteers, helpers, leaders, team members, or something else, we must all recognize that we can't do youth ministry alone. Not only is it not ethical (from a safeguarding perspective), it's simply not possible! In our desire to have enough helpers to run sessions, we sometimes opt for what is often referred to as "warm bodies". In other words, anyone will do. Although this is clearly not best practice, we must acknowledge the challenge of finding suitable adults to help out with youth ministry.

The Nail That Never Gets Hammered

In addition to writing or choosing your teaching materials, one of the biggest challenges of discipleship-oriented youth ministry is recruiting appropriate helpers. Recruitment of volunteers must be constant. As soon as you think you have a great team with plenty of helpers, something changes. Steve loves young people and has a heart of gold, but he gets a different job and though he's been leading a small group Bible study for middle school boys, his new hectic schedule means he's no longer available to lead his Thursday night group. Jessica has been hosting a cooking club at the youth centre for five years, but she's just found out – to her joy and your congratulations – that she's pregnant, so she'll need to take a three-year break from youth work while she and her husband adjust to family life.

As I write this, Covid-19 is wreaking havoc on my volunteer teams. In the span of a few weeks, I had to recruit and replace an entire team of more than half a dozen people for one of my open youth club sessions. Two couples moved out of the area, and four more individuals had to stop serving because of health needs and had to minimize their risk of exposure. All that to illustrate the point: we can never get too comfortable in our volunteer teams. Even when it appears we have enough, we need to be looking out for the next person or couple that you want to ask to join your team. Recruiting volunteer helpers is like the nail that never gets hammered. No matter how long you've been hacking away, it just never goes all the way in. Seasons change. Needs change. Situations change. There is always a need for more people to join the work.

I grew up in a very working-class area in small-town Oklahoma. A typical characteristic of men in my region was that you didn't ask for help. DIY ("do it yourself") wasn't just a section in the hardware store, it was a way of life. No matter what the challenge was, you had to figure it out and do it yourself. You changed your own oil in your car, and maybe even the brakes too if you had the right equipment. This mentality does *not* translate to youth ministry. I have to work hard to get rid of the blue-collar DIY mentality I grew up with. I'll go even further than that. The do-it-yourself mentality in youth ministry is destructive. Based on pride, it reveals a neglect to humble ourselves and ask for help. Or worse, perhaps we secretly like being the person who does everything, meanwhile creating an unhealthy dynamic of a co-dependent relationship with those in our ministerial care.

In youth ministry, we are constantly asking for help. One of the most challenging things I do in my current role is to phone people up and ask them to pray about getting involved in youth ministry. If I'm honest, I dread it. I don't know why it's so difficult to pick up the phone, punch in the numbers, and ask someone to join my team. The worst that can happen is they'll politely say, "No." Don't be like me. Be like Jesus. Although he didn't need the help, per se, he was always asking people to join him in his mission. Asking others for help isn't just about us. By asking others to get involved, we are inviting them into the blessing of getting involved in what God is doing in the lives of young people. I've had multiple interactions with people who were initially resistant to getting involved in youth work. A common response I get is, "I'm too old." One of these men, however, has come to really enjoy spending time with the young people, and he is now one of my biggest supporters.

What are You Looking for?

One of the first things you need to establish when recruiting helpers is, what is it that you're looking for? What do you want them to do? There are different types of volunteer roles and there are different types of volunteers. It's worth thinking through what kind of role you're looking to fill when you consider asking someone to serve. I find that very often people talk themselves out of getting involved in youth ministry before they've had a chance to hear what it involves. Time and time again I've gone to make that phone call, or caught someone after church over coffee, to sound them out about getting involved in youth ministry, only to have them confess to me that they didn't think they were a suitable candidate. In their own reckoning, they were too old, or didn't have any skills with young people, or couldn't teach, or... fill in the blank. After acknowledging their concerns, I gently explain, "I'm just looking for someone who can do twice a month in the snack bar – serving drinks and chocolate bars, and giving change." All of a sudden their expression changes and it dawns on them, "Oh, I could do that!"

So what are you looking for? Someone to lead a Middle Space discussion group weekly? Someone to greet young people at the door and sign them in or out? Someone to give change in the snack shop? All of these are very different roles and require different levels of skill and commitment. With those thoughts in mind, let's consider what goes into joining a youth ministry team as an adult helper. We'll look at the request for helpers through the following three criteria: the Role, Frequency, and Duration.

The first consideration is what *Role* you are looking to fill. Although they may be flexible, each role is different. You need to ask yourself what skills are needed to fill each role, and what is expected in that role. Each volunteer needs to know what it means to be successful or effective in that role. Do they need any special skills (teaching/public speaking, sports, first aid, food preparation, etc.)? Do they need to arrive early or be prepared to stay late? All of this needs to be spelled out as clearly as possible from the beginning. In fact, each role should have its own job description. The last thing volunteers want is to turn up to youth group not really knowing what they are supposed to be doing. The job description doesn't have to be lengthy or overly formal. Generally speaking, one page or less should be enough to cover what is needed. I've found that people are more likely to say "yes" when they know what they are agreeing to. Of course, we also want to bear in mind here our considerations from the previous chapter on using the gifts and talents that people bring to the table. This is where having a good amount of flexibility comes into play.

In addition to the specified role, the next question is in regard to *Frequency*. In past roles where I've served, it was assumed that most youth ministry volunteers would serve weekly. While some might serve on Sundays (teaching Sunday school or leading worship) and others on Wednesdays (small group leaders, registration, etc.), it was still assumed they would serve weekly. No one ever stated this, it was just "part of the furniture", so to speak. In my current rural youth ministry, we've found it helpful to schedule volunteers at a frequency that works for them. For a very few, this still means weekly. For others, it's every other week or even once a month. In rare cases, I have a few volunteers who serve less frequently than that – some don't serve regularly but they're happy for me to phone them up if I'm short for one reason or another. When you first informally interview a potential volunteer, in addition to discussing the role(s) you're looking to fill, talk to them early on about frequency. Many adults may want to bless your ministry but simply cannot commit to serving every week, due to family commitments or career needs. Let's not miss out on good people simply because we haven't discussed a realistic frequency that works for all involved. Of course, the downside is that less frequent volunteers automatically means a need for a greater number of volunteers (one person serving weekly = two people serving fortnightly = four people serving once a month, and so forth). However, I've also found that less frequent serving means keeping a volunteer for longer, as you lower the risk of burnout in youth ministry.

This brings us to our third consideration, which is the *Duration*. This is an important item to discuss with potential new helpers. In other words, how long are you asking them to serve? Many volunteers, who are otherwise excited about supporting the youth work, may be put off if they think they are committing themselves to youth work forever! Here it is worth thinking through a trial period. Make it clear to the candidate the trial is just as much for them as it is for you. You could say something like, "Let's try this for three months and see how it goes. Why don't we speak again next term and you can let me know how you're finding it?" It puts the potential helper at ease because they're only committing for three months, not for the rest of their lives. If three months is too short, make it longer. The exact length isn't as important as the openness of communication, and a fair set of expectations.

The trial period serves as a safety net for both of you. If the helper finds youth work too stressful, or it just isn't right for them, no problem. At the same time, it's a safeguard for you and the youth ministry as well. Perhaps they weren't as warm and friendly towards young people as you expected they would be. Or you find out about some inappropriate language or behaviours they seem unwilling to change. The trial period gives you a shortened time frame in which to act and to communicate that clearly. Whatever you agree to, stick to it. The volunteer will appreciate your level of follow-through when you arrange the promised conversation at the end of the trial period.

At the conclusion of the trial period, make sure to arrange contact with the volunteer within a week of its completion. Arrange a time to meet, or at a minimum to speak by phone. This kind of conversation cannot be had by email or text message, so resist the temptation to shortcut here. The conversation can function as an informal evaluation, but keep it light and positive. Start by asking them what they enjoyed about the last few months serving in youth ministry. You can include questions like these:

- What did you enjoy most about youth ministry?
- What did you enjoy the least?
- What surprised you about working with young people?
- How did you find the frequency and commitment level?
- Evaluate your own role in the youth work. Were there things you would do differently? Would you like to do more, or was it just right?

You can help give them feedback on these questions as well. Avoid approaching these like a checklist, and aim for an informal and warm conversation. Be sure to thank them for serving and for taking the time to talk. You'll want to finish by asking them how they feel about moving forward. If they're happy to continue, then congratulations! You've just gained a new long-term volunteer. On the other hand, if they don't want to continue, thank them for their time and investment in young people, and ask them to commit to regular prayer for yourself and the team. Most importantly, don't be discouraged! Youth ministry isn't for everyone, and you'd much rather have a helper who truly wants to be there.

The Elephant in the Room

Have you ever heard the phrase "the elephant in the room"? It refers to an issue that is so big, and so glaringly obvious, yet everyone is afraid to bring it up – perhaps for fear that no one else sees it – so they tiptoe around it and never talk about it. I feel like ageism is the elephant in the room for youth work. Why do most churches assume that youth leaders need to be young twenty-somethings? Don't get me wrong. I'm eternally grateful for young, energetic, enthusiastic youth leaders. Being only a few years older than the teens we serve gives them a unique perspective and the cultural bridge is much shorter. It can also be problematic. How many stories do you know of youth leaders becoming romantically involved with members of the youth group – often secretly? The temptation was stronger because of the closeness in age, despite the fact that it may have been inappropriate – or worse, illegal! The point here is not whether younger or older youth leaders are better or more ideal, but rather that we need to question our assumptions about what a youth leader looks like.

In our rural village, I rely a lot on older folks, people who are retired. Many of them are the opposite of what we normally think of when we think of youth ministry: young, energetic, hip, and cool. We know deep down that isn't really what's important when it comes to helping people walk with Jesus, but we still fall prey to the mentality. Many of my older volunteers make wonderful helpers. They're warm and friendly and love to serve. Because they're retired, they have more time to give to voluntary work, and they often have a strong desire to use the strength and energy they have left for a good cause. Additionally, the wealth of life experiences they have makes them incredibly valuable in interacting with young people. In my current youth ministry setting, most of my volunteers are aged sixty and older. I don't know if that's normal or not, and to be honest, I don't care. I have wonderful, committed helpers who love young people and do a great job at making them feel welcome. Heck, I'm in my forties, which is well beyond the "normal" age range for an employed youth pastor.

Ideally, we'll have a mix of age ranges involved in youth ministry, but this isn't always possible. There are pros and cons to either side of the pendulum. While younger helpers may have lots of energy and a helpful perspective, many of them have other commitments – work, education, or personal relationships – which may mean they have little time to give to voluntary work. People in their thirties and forties can be wonderful in many ways. They have a bit more life experience and maturity in serving the Lord. Yet, their commitments can be even more strained than for those in their twenties, as they have often started families of their own, meaning they're simply not available on evenings and weekends when the majority of youth ministry takes place. Older folks may have more time to give, but sometimes health concerns can be a prohibitive factor. During Covid, this was a detrimental factor to my volunteer teams, as many of them have had to self-isolate. All we're saying here is not to rule out anyone based on age alone. My best youth ministry volunteers have come from a variety of different backgrounds and age ranges, and have fulfilled a wide variety of different roles.

Where and How to Recruit

I wish the recruitment of volunteers was easier. It would be great if we had so many people coming forward to knock on our doors that we had to turn people away, but I've rarely had that happen. Having said that, it's not nearly as difficult as we sometimes make it out to be. Truth be told, we just have to ask. I've found that appeals to the masses very rarely work: an ad or report in the church newsletter, a post on social media, that sort of thing. I've rarely had anyone come forward from things like that – only once or twice in my twenty years of youth ministry. More often than not, I get volunteers by asking them directly.

So, whom do you ask? In Matthew chapter 4, Jesus is led by the Holy Spirit into the desert, during which he experiences a series of temptations from the devil. He had been fasting for forty days and nights. Not long after defeating Satan and returning from his fast, Jesus begins to call his twelve disciples. I've often wondered if the time Jesus spent in prayer and fasting had something to do with the calling of those men who would follow him the closest over the next three years – those who would be his closest companions, his intimate allies on mission. I do not want to understate the importance of prayer when it comes to asking people to help. Ask anyone who's been in youth ministry for a long time – a good volunteer can be a huge blessing to you and the young people you work with; a bad volunteer can make life miserable for you and others, or in extreme cases could be the end of your youth ministry. Don't panic though, the point is the need to seek God about good volunteers (we'll talk more about safeguarding a little bit further on in this chapter).

Sometimes when you've prayed – or even during your prayer – the Holy Spirit might bring a face or a name to your mind. A few years ago, I was looking to build up a particular team in our youth ministry. I'd long had a dream to have a couple who would take on the organization of the cooking and all meal preparation for our annual camps. I had been speaking to our lead pastor about the issue, and he encouraged me to pray about it. Each time I prayed, a particular couple came to mind. I had never asked them to be a part of our camping ministry before, but every time I prayed their names came to the forefront of my mind. I mentioned it to my pastor, and he didn't see any reason not to ask them. This was a big ask. Whoever took on the role would need to be willing to go camping with teenagers. To have the right attitude towards young people. To be able to cope with sleeping under the stars for a weekend. And, on top of that, to have the cooking and planning skills to feed all of us for the whole weekend. In short, I asked them. They thought about it, prayed about it. They accepted it. They have been my core camping team for nearly ten years now. They don't currently do anything else in youth work (weekly sessions, outreach, etc.), but their annual contribution to this particular ministry is worth their weight in gold!

It's not always that clear. I asked two or three other people who said no, before I got that kind of clarity. Other times, I pray and don't get such distinct clarity. James tells us, "You do not have because you do not ask God" (James 4:2). I've also found this to be true with people. Sometimes we just have to ask for help. So another tactic I learned from my pastor is simply praying through the church directory. Get out a copy of your church directory or log in to your church database, then prayerfully go through the names on the list. Many of them will be inappropriate to ask for a number of reasons. Sophie is in her eighties and doesn't get around well due to poor health. Ronald, despite his new life in Christ, will not be able to pass a background check due to some legal trouble he got into before he became a Christian. These are people you want to ask to support the youth ministry through their prayers, but not with their direct involvement. As you rule out the ones you are not going to ask, jot down a short list of "maybes". These are people who are not currently involved in the youth ministry, who are not over-committed to other areas of the church (as far as you know), and who have the basic personal warmth and personality that you would be looking for. If possible, you may want to run this list past your pastor or another church leader who may know the individuals better than you do. Sometimes they may know of reasons not to ask someone of which you are unaware. For instance,

I recently presented such a list to my pastor, which included Joanna. Unbeknownst to me or to the wider church, Joanna had recently taken on a huge responsibility in the church, which would mean her helping out in the youth work would not be possible. Conversely, your list might spark their thoughts and so you wind up adding three or four people to the list.

The next step is to pick up the phone and ask. Make sure you work on your phone etiquette; engage in a little small talk before ploughing right into it. Let them know you are not expecting an answer right then and there. It's a big ask, and a big commitment, so acknowledge they may need some time to think about it. Also, be prepared for roughly half of them to say no. Don't take this personally. Thank them for their time and ask them to pray for the youth ministry. If they are disinterested in volunteering with the youth work, you probably don't want them there anyway. I don't mean that in any kind of snarky way. It's just that youth work can be difficult at times. It takes commitment and a positive attitude. If they feel it isn't right for them, it's likely not!

You can also prepare to be amazed from time to time. Occasionally, a potential volunteer makes it easy. "Have you ever thought about getting involved in youth work?" Then comes the pause, while you bite your nails waiting for a response. The voice on the other end says, "Yes, I have thought about that, and I'd love to get involved." You breathe a sigh of relief, but you're slightly shocked that someone is not only willing but sounds enthusiastic about supporting the youth ministry! I've had quite a few of those calls recently. It makes it that much easier to pick up the phone the next time.

In addition to phone calls and utilizing the church directory, don't underestimate the role of the face-to-face encounter. I know it's our job to hang out with young people most of the time, but at least once or twice per month, rub shoulders with the adults during the after-church coffee time or the fellowship dinner. Getting to know parents, grandparents, couples, or single adults goes a long way. Some volunteers will give their time to a cause they believe in. Others will give their time only when asked specifically. Still others will give their time to an *individual* that they like or feel drawn towards. Personal relationships in this regard are key. A little word of caution here too. Make sure your asking doesn't pose the threat of you becoming the equivalent of a multilevel marketing salesman. Guard those special friendships. Don't ask everyone you meet.

You want some friends in the end who aren't connected to your work. Again, be sure to approach every ask through prayer, and even fasting where appropriate.

It's worth here making a brief observational note about pluralism. So far we have talked mainly about volunteers in regard to church folk. In a church-run ministry – even one that is Middle Space in approach – Christian people will likely make up the majority of your volunteers. For your Christian discipleship or faith-based sessions, this is essential. As we discussed in the last chapter, you want people helping who are modelling the concepts you are teaching. At the same time, a Middle Space approach to youth work should reflect the community in which it serves. It is perfectly acceptable – or even recommended – to employ volunteers in your open youth work (the bridge-building opportunities mentioned in chapter 7) who aren't necessarily Christians. If your project is truly Middle Space, it will be community-oriented. It will also be attempting to meet the various and multifaceted needs of young people in your community. As such, you may find people who are not necessarily following Jesus who yet support your work with young people. This is perfectly reasonable, as long as you both understand the nature of the youth work. Just make sure that they are aware of the nature of the overarching project and its Christian purposes.

Safeguarding and Background Checks

One completely non-negotiable aspect of working with young people is having a system of safeguarding checks and balances in place. I would argue that safeguarding young people from harm or abuse is probably our top priority, probably even above sharing the gospel with them. It does no good to lead a young person to Christ, only to find out they are being harmed in ways that damage them spiritually, psychologically, emotionally, or physically. Harm done in the name of the Church can be of the worst kind. So what kind of checks need to be in place?

The first point of action, and the absolute bare minimum, is to start with a background check. Ideally, your church or sponsoring organization will have someone designated to undertake these checks. In the UK these are known as DBS checks (Disclosure and Barring Services). No one should start volunteering until the background check has been completed and has come back with a favourable result. The *only* exception to this is perhaps one trial visit, in which the potential volunteer *observes* youth work, as opposed to taking part or leading anything. The checks will look into whether there have been any criminal records or any related problems that would bar someone from taking part in youth ministry. There is, of course, a fee for undertaking such checks, which should be covered by the ministry budget. This isn't something to grumble about, rather it's part of the way we express our love to the community and make the safety of young people a top priority!

Although background checks are the beginning of a healthy approach to safeguarding in youth ministry, they are also simply the bare minimum. What we really want to create is an entire atmosphere and ethos where safeguarding and best practice are integrated into the very fabric of the youth work. The next logical step is providing some initial safeguarding training, with the potential for ongoing training and/or renewal. Each volunteer should have a good understanding of each of the following questions:

- How many volunteers/adult helpers are needed for each session? Which roles are essential and how do we manage the logistics, considering our localized setting?
- What constitutes harm? What needs to be reported? Who is my first point of contact if I have a concern about a young person?
- What does confidentiality mean in this setting? Do my volunteers know *not* to promise confidentiality around certain issues that *must* be discussed with the team leader or other authorities?
- How do we build an appropriate and healthy level of trust with young people, while listening to their concerns and offering personal support, without building unhealthy or inappropriate bonds with them?
- How can I best safeguard myself in situations of potential vulnerability?

It is not our purpose in this book to answer all of these questions. Nonetheless, any work with children and young people must take these situations into account. A Middle Space approach to youth work is no different. In fact, because we are working with so many young people not familiar with church, safeguarding becomes even more important because often there may not be direct contact or relationships with parents.

Although recruitment of volunteers is the "nail that never gets hammered", safeguarding requires the same level of diligence and ongoing attention. As we said above, it is one of the most important things we do in youth ministry. And yet, it is also something that often goes without notice, because if it's done right, there is nothing to see. This axiom holds a lot of truth: "When safeguarding goes right, no one notices. When it goes wrong, everyone will know about it."

Reflection Section

What do you think about this statement: "Youth ministry is not DIY"?

Think about a youth leader who made a positive impact on you. Why does that person stick out to you? What attributes did they have?

Consider your own safeguarding practices, or those you have observed in another ministry. What is being done well? What could be done better? What changes need to be made immediately in order to make your youth work safer for young people and the adults serving them?

9

Making Middle Space Sustainable

It's a well-known truism that most paid youth ministers only stay in post for an average of eighteen months. I've found this to be true, at least anecdotally, on both sides of the Atlantic. There are a whole host of reasons for this. One of them is that the changing nature of youth culture means adults working with young people need to constantly reinvent themselves and/or their youth ministry practices. Let's be honest: this can be exhausting, especially for those of us who struggle with change. Youth culture is constantly changing, and therefore aspects of our work with them will constantly be changing. This barrage of constant change gets tiring, leading some youth workers to throw in the towel after a year or two. Although this is understandable (even my first youth ministry role lasted only a year), we must also consider that a constantly revolving door of youth leaders weakens the long-term stability of a youth ministry, and the potential for a long-term positive impact on the lives of the young people. Hypothetically, if the eighteen-month turnover trend was to continue, a young person might have a total of five lead youth workers throughout a seven-year stint in a church's youth ministry. We, as a Church, as the larger body of Christians working with young people, need to ask ourselves a very important question: how can we make youth ministry more sustainable and give youth workers a better chance for long-term success?

Organizational Structure and Supervision

In an earlier chapter, we talked about the dangers of basing success in youth ministry on numbers only. This implies a need to create new metrics of success in Christian youth work. While it's all well and good to talk about redefining success in youth ministry, it's not enough to simply move away from a numbers-based approach. Indeed, moving away from a "more bums in pews" mentality is essential, but it might be only the first step. We spent earlier chapters talking a lot about models of youth ministry, and how important it is to define what it is you do and why you do it, but most of that discussion was focused on the lead youth worker in a setting. We've also talked about how often the approach to youth ministry follows the ministry model in the sponsoring church or organization (at the very least the two need to be in harmony). What will also become clearer to the reader is the need for clear communication and expectation from your supervisor, line manager, or others in positions of leadership or power to which you report. In other words, is everyone on the same page about the key factors in your youth ministry? This goes for the lead youth worker, key volunteers, but also for those in positions of supervision and oversight. A youth worker may have a well thought out vision for youth work, and a clearly defined understanding of what makes for success, but this broader vision needs to be shared by the higher-ups.

Let's say you're starting a new youth ministry position and you have a heart for outreach into the local community. You're aware that building a programme of youth ministry that takes outreach seriously will take time, and that immediate results are unlikely. You've come to accept that and are committed to a long-term approach to youth ministry in a way that impacts the wider community. Is your lead pastor (or other supervisor) on the same page with you? Will they allow you the freedom to redefine success in youth ministry beyond, "We want more young people in church on Sunday mornings"? Some lengthy discussions will need to take place with senior church leaders, denominational leaders, youth organizations, and key youth workers on the ground regarding long-term goals, expectations, and management of both. My hope is that church leaders are reading this book in addition to, or even alongside, youth leaders, and you're both able to work through the deeper questions of your philosophy of ministry to young people and the goals and expectations around it.

In my observation of youth work in both the United States and the United Kingdom, it is clear that there are often vast disparities between what a youth worker hopes to accomplish and what the senior church leader/supervisor wants to see accomplished. I attended a youth work conference a few years ago where one of the speakers was a senior church leader. His talk was on "What youth leaders need to know about pastors", or something to that effect. One of his ten points was humorously titled,

"The youth minister exists to make the senior pastor look good." When he read that line out, the crowd was immediately divided into those who laughed at the humorous, partially valid point, and those who groaned at the pain it invoked. I have certainly worked in at least one location where his statement rang 100 per cent true. I've also worked in locations where there was a genuine desire to reach out to young people in incarnational and missional ways. The problem is that so often neither the youth minister nor the lead pastor is aware of each other's hidden expectations, nor are they able to have an open conversation about them. I'm hoping that this book will facilitate some discussion around the issues of vision, philosophy of ministry, goals, and expectations.

When there is clarity of purpose and expectations, there follows the right balance between freedom and guidance. Youth workers (and, in fact, those in any other associate leadership role) inherently need to meet regularly or semi-regularly with their line manager. How often this is done depends on the setting, needs, and relationship, but I would argue that once a month is not enough. What we are trying to achieve is the right balance between the freedom to do youth work in the way it needs to be done (that is, according to the clearly defined vision and goals), and the occasional guidance needed from a supervisor or line manager. Everyone needs input from someone in higher authority from time to time. Even lead pastors need to be receiving wisdom, guidance, and accountability from someone.

Although it may not be practical in every setting, I recommend meeting with your supervisor or manager weekly (with the occasional break for holidays or other uncommon disruptions). A good practice to start with is asking a few basic questions every time you meet. The first is, "How did it go last week (or since we last met)?" At this point, you bring up any items that need to be discussed. Thinking back over your last week working with young people, were there any disciplinary issues that had to be addressed, or any injuries to attend to? Any difficult conversations with parents or young people? Did you encounter any young people who need additional support? This conversation helps build long-term trust and gives an added layer of accountability. As a youth worker, your supervisor should never hear of a surprise, or something eventful that happened, from someone else.

The second question is, "Do you need anything from me?" This is an extension of the first question, but leads into areas in which you may need support. Was there a particularly difficult conversation – one in which it would be helpful to get an outside perspective? Do you need help handling a situation with a difficult volunteer? It can also include the practical: forms that need signing, expense claims to process and get paid, permissions for offsite trips or events, etc. There will be some weeks when there is nothing to discuss here, but because you are having the conversation regularly, it means that not only are there no surprises, but also you have the support you need.

Whereas the first two questions look backwards, the third question looks ahead: "What do you have coming up (in the next week or further) that I need to know about?" Again, this can touch on the practical, or otherwise. Do you need to have a difficult conversation for which it would be really useful to have prayer covering? Are you attending a seminar or conference, and you need your boss to remember that you won't be in the office two days next week? Do you have an extra ministry engagement – something out of the ordinary for which you'd like prayer support or logistical help? Perhaps you're speaking at a nearby youth event or leading a school assembly or outreach ministry, in addition to your normal ministry responsibilities. These are all examples of things to discuss here.

Finally, you take time to pray together. You'll want to pray through those issues that you've discussed using the above questions. However, you'll also pray for your supervisor. As appropriate, he or she will share issues for prayer with you as well. This is a great way to build trust, improve your working relationship, and also keep the long-term ministry vision in front of both of you. Because you are talking together and praying together weekly (or as regularly as possible), you will be continually relating to one another around the needs of the ministry, but also personally as co-laborers in Christ, working together towards similar goals. You may also choose to do this with a shared meal or at least over coffee or tea.

Years ago when I worked in a larger church, sadly there was not this kind of supervisory relationship. Our large pastoral team got together once per month for lunch together, followed by a lengthy devotional led by the senior pastor. Don't get me wrong, the lead pastor had an incredible amount of biblical knowledge and wisdom to share with the rest of us. But unfortunately, I never felt like I got to know the pastor I was working for. Although I did have a supervisory relationship with another senior staff member, our meetings were more ad hoc, or on an "as needed" basis. By contrast, in my current role, I meet together with my lead pastor in precisely the way I described above. Although the two of us are very different people, we gather together around shared goals and shared ministry. It has largely revolutionized the way I see ministry leadership and supervising others.

Managing Oneself

If you want to have a sustainable youth ministry, in other words, one that can last for a long time and continue to bear fruit throughout its life cycle, one of the most important issues you can address is managing one's own self. We discussed the merits and absolute necessity of safe-guarding policies and procedures, in regard to keeping young people safe and protected. Safeguarding, however, also protects the adults working with young people, by not allowing them to get into awkward or precarious situations. It helps keep us out of vulnerable situations, and also safeguards us against the potential for wrongful allegations, which are rare but nonetheless do occur.

Safeguarding, however, is only the tip of the iceberg when it comes to managing ourselves. Another way we can self-manage has to do with setting healthy boundaries for ourselves and agreed expectations with our supervisor. Do you have a clearly defined workweek? Do you know how many hours you are expected to work and is it clearly defined in your contract? Perhaps out of my morbid sense of curiosity, I occasionally like to browse through youth work job postings, just to see what is out there, so to speak. I recently came across a youth ministry position advertised in the United States, in which the work expectations were set at 55 hours a week. Let's think about this for a moment. If the normal full-time workweek hovers around 40 hours per week (give or take a few hours), this contract was for 15 hours above that – or essentially two full days' work! I won't tell you what words I wanted to mumble under my breath when I read that. Sometimes churches can be much further behind general work practices and labour policies found in the secular market. We need to do better.

Let's say you have a much more realistic workweek, with a contract for 40 hours a week, give or take. Who is monitoring your hours? Most of us won't have an old-fashioned time clock to punch us in and out. Do you keep track of your own hours, or is someone else monitoring it? I find that very often, we youth workers – because of our passion for seeing God work in the lives of young people – will work more than our allotted hours. A few years ago, I started keeping track of my own hours, just as an experiment. I wanted to see how many hours a week I was actually working, but I also wanted to see where most of my time was going. In my case, I found I was spending too much time attempting social media networking with young people and with our official youth centre pages, and not enough time praying and preparing sessions. What would your spreadsheet look like?

In addition to setting boundaries around the number of hours we log, we youth workers need to consider our own expectations of ourselves, and what we are able to accomplish. About ten years ago, our youth centre went through a phase where our Thursday night session for older teens (fifteen to eighteen) was really blowing up and had become the cool place to hang out. Bear in mind, none of these teenagers were walking with Jesus. This was an open youth club session and for whatever reason, we were getting large groups of teens from a slightly rougher crowd. While this was incredible, it was also eye-opening. As I started to get to know these kids, I was exposed to more of their world and what they were up to. I picked up on things from their conversations with me and with one another, that they often didn't realize I was perceiving. Their faces kept me awake at night. This session ended at 10:00 p.m. which is fairly late for a youth session. But these were the kinds of kids who would have stayed out until 11:00 or 12:00, even on a school night, just so they could be together and out of the house. And strangely enough, their parents didn't seem to mind them being out late. Even finishing as late as 10:00, I'd stay afterwards and pray – and often worry – for and about them.

Sometimes, as I made that one-mile drive back up to my house, I'd see a small group of them out on the corner next to the shop. Because I took such ownership of the youth work – and of them personally – rather than going home to bed, I'd go out on the corner with them, just to get in a few more minutes of relational ministry. If I'm honest, it was partially motivated by fear. What kind of trouble were they going to get in *if I'm not with them*? You can see where this is going. I was taking on too much responsibility for the lives of these young people. Don't get me wrong, there is something beautiful and holy about caring for these young people in the way that I did. There is also something dangerous and self-destructive. In my desire to be there for the young people, had I forgotten that it's the Lord's work? It's not up to me to save them, or even to keep them out of trouble. It's only up to me to represent Christ as best I can, when I am with them. Further to the point, without realizing it, I was violating my own safeguarding principles by doing detached youth work on my own, late at night. Fortunately, since then I've been able to set much healthier boundaries for myself. I still care about young people. Heck, I even still worry about them. I see their faces when my head hits my pillow. I'm still learning to trust God for his work in their lives.

A most common and very subtle danger when learning to manage ourselves involves our own friendships. This is a tricky one to balance. In Middle Space youth work, we spend a lot of our time with young people. We present ourselves, to a degree, as someone on their level. Someone they can relate to. Someone who is a friend. There is a subtle danger here when we also begin to view them as our friends, or when we begin to have our own social or emotional needs met by young people. Can young people be our friends? Absolutely! But they must not be our only friends – nor should they be our peers. A few years ago, my wife asked me: "Loyd, who are your friends?" I fumbled around, struggled with the question, and named one or two. But I was noticing that in my heart, I wanted to say, "The youth group are my friends!" It's not that I was wrong about that; young people can indeed be our friends. However, I was in danger of over-identifying with the young people in an unhealthy way.

One of the biggest assets you can have to help you manage yourself and keep healthy boundaries is your own set of adult friends. If possible, tap into any local youth work support groups, prayer sessions, regional groups, etc. Attend every youth worker meeting that you can. If none exist in your area, then help create them. It doesn't matter if it's two people or twenty-two, you will benefit greatly from sharing stories, prayers, and life together. There is also a lot to be said for having friends that don't have anything at all to do with youth work. Friends you've known for years, or new friends you've acquired through your local setting or a shared interest.

On that note, personal interests and hobbies are another great way to help you manage yourself and set healthy boundaries. What do you really enjoy doing? What sort of physical activities do you like? What about art and entertainment? Do you still have time to do them in light of your current work responsibilities? If not, I would argue that is unhealthy. We all have busy seasons where we don't have much time for extracurricular activities. In the week running up to a camp or retreat, you might not have time for mountain biking. When a crisis hits a family in your ministry, it's probably not the time to suggest a Harry Potter marathon. However, if you haven't had time for your hobby or personal passion for a while, then you need to take a look at your priorities and personal boundaries.

I love to ask pastors and youth workers, "When is your day off?" While many of them are increasingly able to give me a clear answer, every once in a while I meet someone who is unable to identify their Sabbath. Let me say this loud and clear: you need one day every week in which you do not do *any* work. You don't check emails. You don't answer the phone (unless you know it's family or friends). You don't buy chocolate for the snack bar. You don't plan next week's teaching lesson. And here's a controversial one: if you have Sunday responsibilities at your church, this is not a day off. Many of us in Christian youth ministry will have work responsibilities on a Sunday, meaning we will need to have another day off during the week. Sadly, some youth workers are not encouraged to count their Sunday responsibilities as work hours, but rather to see them as a "gift to the church". Let's be clear about this: if you are *required* to be there, it's work. It is not for someone else to tell you what your gift to the church should be.

Your Sabbath is yours. Jesus said, "The Sabbath was made for man, not man for the Sabbath" (Mark 2:27). Your day off is a day to recharge, and reconnect with the Lord. It's a day to sleep in if you want to – or to get up early and go exploring for fun. A day to read and relax, or take a walk on the beach or through the woods. A day to spend time with your spouse or your family, to catch up on your favourite sports team, or to watch a few episodes of that new series. My days off are often spent listening to obscure indie rock on vinyl – and then, of course, posting pictures of it on social media! What your day off should not involve, however, is anything related to youth work or your church. Of course, there are exceptions. You get a phone call regarding a true emergency. Or there is a weekend retreat that straddles your normal day off. These must be the exceptions rather than the rule, and when working on your normal day off is necessary, you should plan carefully to take time off another day that week. My current supervisor is very good at holding me to this. "Loyd, you've got a camping trip this weekend. Which day earlier in the week are you going to take off since you're working on Friday?" This is precisely how we should be looking out for each other in kingdom work – not simply asking how much we can get from one another.

Career Trajectory

There's one final area we need to discuss regarding sustainable youth work, and that is regarding the career trajectory of those doing youth ministry. Another well-known stereotype in youth ministry is that it is often used as a "stepping stone" to get experience for other types of ministry. Not all careers look alike, and it is certainly acceptable for people to alter their career trajectories as they go along. Some enter youth ministry because it seems a logical step in getting ministry experience before going into other forms of pastoral ministry, work with adults, associate roles, etc. However, sometimes this view can be detrimental both to healthy youth ministry and to a healthy career path. I knew a man who once admitted he hated working with teenagers, and yet he started his ministry career in youth work. Why? He saw no other way to get real-life ministry experience while preparing for his call to the pastorate. As horrible as this sounds, the blame does not solely lie with the individual. Church structures and denominations need to be better organized when it comes to ministry training, internships, curacies, and the like.

In the preceding chapter, we talked about the question of age in regard to youth work. Although it's true that there isn't an age limit on youth work, there are very real limitations – or at least changes to be made – in how we do youth ministry as we get older. As we get older, our family needs change, which often means our financial needs change. I know many youth workers who have wanted to stay employed in youth ministry for much longer, but they could not afford to do so. Their job did not pay them a living wage, or due to budgetary cutbacks at their organization, they were reduced to part-time hours. I'm afraid I don't have any answers here, just more questions. There are much bigger, systemic issues with the overlap of Church, finance, human resources, and youth ministry that we are not equipped to deal with in this book. Nonetheless, it is important for us as individual youth workers to give some serious thought, prayer, and discussion to our own career trajectories.

I remember being young and naïve and thinking, "I'll simply trust God and go where he sends me, and stay there until he sends me somewhere else." Although that line of thinking is not wrong and may even be admirable, it is also too simplistic. Let me encourage youth workers everywhere to consider their own long-term goals. This includes not only their youth ministry goals, but their own career goals, family goals, and financial goals. Where would you like to see yourself in five years? Ten years? And beyond? Are there training courses you could take that would make it easier to justify a pay increase next year? Can you seek out an extra qualification: anything from practical training like a first aid course, to an academic degree, or even an advanced degree? Those of you who are good with words could try submitting an article or Bible study guide for publication in a specialized youth ministry periodical. These challenges help keep our minds fresh and sharp, and also may contribute to our income, or open doors to future opportunities.

As you consider your five-year or ten-year plan, it's worth asking yourself: if you had to stop doing what you are doing right now, what else would you want to do? What career and/or ministry passions would you pursue if you didn't have any of the limitations of your current role? When it's all said and done, remind yourself that you matter to God just as much as the young people you serve. Let's make sure we're believing the message that we are delivering to others. Conversely, you may answer that by saying, "I would continue to do exactly what I am doing now." If that's the case, what extra support, finance, training, or freedom do you need to keep doing it in a healthy and sustainable way?

Succession Planning and Teamwork

While we've already addressed the crucial role that volunteers can play in the youth work itself, there is another reason to build a good team. The DIY mindset is destructive in youth work not only because it's unsustainable for yourself, but also because of the potential for safeguarding issues. It also sets up the youth ministry to depend on one person, so when (not if) that person leaves for any number of reasons, who is left to carry the youth work into the future? An unhealthy transition can occur resulting in heartbreak and emotional devastation when young people or parents have been encouraged to put too much faith into the person leading the youth work.

Aside from the negative situations we want to avoid, there are many positive reasons for building a good team. First, having the right people around you, supporting the youth work, can allow the youth ministry to serve others in ways that one person alone never can. There are talents and gifts on your team that you and I simply do not have. How can we make use of these individuals in a way that is both satisfying to the individual using their talents, and also beneficial to the youth ministry? As lead youth workers, we should be in the business of equipping and empowering others around us. Sometimes we do a pretty good job of this with the young people themselves: recognizing a call on a young person's life, or developing their talents in music, speaking, sports, or something else. We should also be doing this with our adult team(s).

Another reason for developing the gifts of your team members has to do with succession. Think for a moment: what would happen to your sessions with young people if (God forbid) something happened to you tomorrow? Would everything have to stop, or do you have key people that could carry on the work temporarily until a suitable replacement was found? It's not a nice thought, perhaps, to think about such a quick exit, but it's a great exercise in helping us to think about what we need to do to make our work more sustainable, even after we're gone.

So how do we plan for succession? That might sound complicated or intimidating, but actually it's quite simple. First, we have to start now. Don't put it off until you've been offered a job somewhere else, or you decide to move back closer to family. At that point, it might be too late. Starting now might simply involve deliberately taking some time off when your sessions are in place. When my own children have had a dance recital or a soccer game out of town, my supervisor has often encouraged me to take time to go and support them, even if it meant missing a youth session. Besides the obvious benefit of me getting to spend time with my children, these instances provide opportunities to equip others to do the work when I'm gone. They serve as mini-experiments for you to train and develop your team for when there are bigger needs: like when you have a medical emergency that requires you to take significant time off, or some other scenario.

Start by thinking through all of the roles that are needed to run a single session, including your own. Second, what are the things that you do that no one else knows about? This might include things like having the right keys to any doors accessed during your session – not just the main door but any storage closets, file cabinets, etc. It will also include very minor things that you probably do without realizing it: taking out the rubbish at the end of the night, washing up dishes, taking home any towels or cloths to be washed, restocking the drinks in the snack shop, or cashing out the money box. It will also include bigger items: appointing someone to run the games or activities and to deliver any teaching relevant to your session.

Time spent developing your team members is never time lost. Not only is it helpful in planning for succession, but it is time devoted to building up the kingdom of God. Ten people doing the work of the ministry is more advantageous over the long term than one person attempting to do it all themselves. Yes, it takes longer to train someone to do something that you can do blindfolded, but that is not the point. When others serve, they learn to use the gifts and talents that God has given them. As they do this, others in turn learn to use their gifts and talents, creating a culture of empowerment and blessing. When we're careful to build up others and equip them for service in the kingdom, we leave behind a wide wake of kingdom-minded people serving their communities in the name of Christ.

Reflection Section

What are the metrics of success in the youth ministry you lead or take part in (or supervise)? Is everyone in unity concerning this vision? Are there any conversations you need to have regarding these things?

We mentioned three areas in which we need to manage ourselves: healthy boundaries, personal friendships and interests, and keeping a personal Sabbath. Which of these areas do you struggle with the most? What are some steps you could take to address it?

Spend some time thinking about your long-term goals. Where do you see yourself in five years? Be sure to think about ministry goals (in youth work), personal career goals, financial goals, and family goals. What about in ten years' time? Is there anything that needs to change now in order to help you achieve these goals?

What plans have you made for succession? What steps still need to be taken to ensure a seamless transition in youth work if/when you leave your position?

10

What's Next?

I can hear many of your brain gears turning. Some of you are celebrating the idea of a new model. Others of you are (rightly) recognizing it's not all that new, just a realigning of some priorities and ways of doing things. Yet others are grumbling. Not because you're angry, or unconvinced of the principles of Middle Space. Rather, it's because you are convinced there's something here and you don't know where or how to start.

Many of you are in churches or sponsoring organizations where a complete reboot just isn't feasible, or even wise. If you are serving in a church where the dominant ministry model is Attractional, it's unlikely you'll be able to convince your whole church leadership to shift to a missional model like Middle Space. In fact, it may not even be healthy to attempt such a turnaround. Correspondingly, it is also unlikely that a fully Middle Space youth ministry could function as the main provision for youth at an Attractional church. However, it might be possible for an Attractional church to sponsor or endorse a Middle Space youth project as an outreach venture of the church. Others of you may be working primarily in Detached youth work settings. Are there ways to integrate some of the principles and practices of Middle Space into your existing missional youth work?

How Can We Create Middle Space?

The most obvious way to approach Middle Space is by utilizing a separate facility. This is where your hopes, dreams, and prayers align and grow some legs. For our centre in England, a number of things aligned at just the right time that meant running Christian youth work in a dedicated youth centre just made sense. I don't think anyone could have planned that, it was a sort of miracle composed of the right timing and right people and ideas all coming together at once. I hope and pray that kind of miracle is able to happen for some of you. For others, it might take a little more effort.

If God is calling you to Middle Space youth work, it is worth spending some time driving through your town, city, or rural area, eyes open, praying and looking for spaces that might be suitable for a Middle Space project. It may also be time to pick up the phone and make some calls to people in your network who know commercial real estate, particularly if they are sympathetic to your cause. Have a conversation with your local government authority or representative and explain to them what you want to do. You might have twenty of these conversations before you find the one that leads you somewhere, but I have found that the more we ask, the more we get. Get key people in your church or ministry praying and asking for favour, for networking contacts, and for guidance on how to approach things. Keep your eyes open for empty buildings and reclaimable spaces, bearing in mind that location is everything. As you start to narrow in on a few spots, ask questions like:

- Are young people already present in this area?
- Is it easily accessible and exposed to foot traffic?
- Is the building structurally sound or will it need lots of expensive repairs?
- Do you have people who believe in what you are doing who would help manage a renovation project?

Nothing good ever happens without some degree of effort. Even in our case, once we agreed to take on the building for a youth centre, there was still lots of work to be done. The building had sat empty for a long time and many improvements were needed. It was not up to date with safety codes, disabled access, and all sorts of issues. However, the partnership between the local church and local parish council meant that the funds could be raised and allocated to the project. Because the vision was clear and well-communicated, the community (even those outside the church family) got behind the project and it came together in under a year.

Creating Middle Space Without a Separate Facility

In case you missed it, Middle Space is not primarily about the repudiation of sacred spaces, as much as it's about widening out what we mean by "sacred space" and getting really creative and innovative in our use of ministry spaces. Furthermore, Middle Space is as much about the concept of meeting young people in the middle – in a neutral ground, or shared space. This has as much to do with our attitude and approach to ministry with young people as it has to do with the physical space. In my current rural context, we are blessed with having a dedicated youth centre that is physically separate from the main church building (just over a mile away), and yet it's run by the church. But what about those who are working in contexts where there is not an abundance of buildings, nor space in general? What might Middle Space look like in an urban setting, for instance, where they don't have access to playing fields or woodland? What could it look like in an existing church facility without a separate building down the road? Can Middle Space be created or reimagined within church facilities that also serve other age groups or purposes? Of course it can!

Although the most natural way to approach Middle Space ministry and outreach is in a dedicated space, separate from the main sacred space/ church building, not everyone will be able to rush out and buy or lease a new facility for Middle Space purposes. Even though I hope that some of you are thinking in that kind of radical direction, for some it just won't be feasible. We are going to look more in-depth at specific locations utilizing several different approaches to Middle Space, but let's consider here a few ways to do Middle Space within an existing church facility.

Does your church or ministry have rooms or space that could be set aside solely for Middle Space youth work? Let's entertain a few ideas, many of which I have observed in actual churches (and a few hypothetical ones):

- A spare Sunday school class is redecorated to create a more inviting, less "churchy" environment.
- The basement floor of a church is gutted and renovated to become a café, with a full coffee bar. A stage is built for live music performances, where both local and touring artists perform. The café has its own name/identity and a separate entrance, creating a true Middle Space between the church and those they are trying to reach.
- A church with a gym opens up the sports facility for sessions other than simply before/after church. Activities include competitions, tournaments, and even some informal instruction or training in basketball, volleyball, indoor soccer, etc. (depending on the skills of available helpers).

- In an artistic or musical community, a church dedicates a whole room to creative expression. Young people invite their friends to open mic sessions, art exhibits, or open sessions to create, paint, sculpt, etc. Regular and ongoing creative classes are offered by local artists.
- A weekly board games night creates a small community of intense strategic gamers in a room or space dedicated to facilitating a missional relationship. Alternatively, a similar space could be used for video games or LAN (local area network) parties.
- Some former teachers or tutors feel led to start a homework club in the church. Once a week (or as often as they can), they open a room in the church to assist young people who are struggling with their grades in particular subjects, or to help them achieve success in their exams.
- A church in a mountainous region doesn't have any spare space in the church at all, but they have a few adults who are gifted in outdoor sports and recreation. So they start a mountain biking club, offer free kayaking lessons, or start a weekly rock climbing club, creating Middle Space in the great outdoors, rather than in any church building.

What we need to be clear about here is the difference in scope between a Middle Space approach to youth work, and an events-based Attractional approach. The above are examples of ways to integrate aspects of Middle Space ministry – that is, long-term missional-based approaches to building community and connecting people who do not yet follow Christ with those who already know and love the Lord. These events would be for the purpose of building long-term relationships, not one-off events to simply attract young people through the doors of the church.

How does one choose which of these ideas to pursue? A number of key factors need to be considered. The first is your local culture. What are the needs in your area? Do kids need safe spaces in which to play sports and socialize? Or is there a need for free academic help? Are you in a community with lots of interest in the arts, music, drama, etc.? It's important to look not only at the needs, but also the strengths, the gifts, and the prospects. In which of these areas can you create a Middle Space missional environment that truly connects to the local culture?

The second thing to consider is: what kinds of gifts and strengths do you have in terms of people resources? This is where your prayer-networking is going to come to the forefront. Do you have church members (or others in your community) who might be willing to teach an art class, book gigs, host the coffee bar, or run the sports sessions? What gifts, talents, or personal passions do you yourself possess that could transform the way youth ministry is done in your local context? I am hopeless at any kind of art or creativity, but I love running outdoor strategic wide games, which we have used a lot in our youth work. However, I have individuals on my team who are gifted at art and creative expression, whom we have empowered to lead Saturday morning art spaces.

This leads us to our third consideration when trying to decide what kind of Middle Space project to adopt. What spaces or facilities do you have that could be used for Middle Space youth work? This is where you really need to look at all of the angles and possibilities, and think outside of the box. Some Middle Space projects do not require any building space at all. Is your church/ministry near to a community park, where you could play flag football or ultimate Frisbee regularly? On the other hand, maybe your church has the ubiquitous "storage room" that is overrun with ancient books or supplies that haven't been used in over a decade? Could that space be better allocated for ministry use?

There is not necessarily a sequential order to how each of these three considerations is dealt with: local culture, people resources, and available space. How you proceed will largely depend on finding the right combination of the three things. I myself am passionate about music. I've always imagined trying to create a Middle Space environment that had the feel of a hip record store or live music venue. When the Lord called us to England, I requested for a stage to be built in the youth centre, hoping that we'd be able to use it for gigs and open mic sessions. However, in rural Sussex, that just wasn't part of the culture. I hosted two to three gigs that very few people attended and realized it just wasn't meant to be. In our context, we got a lot more mileage out of the outdoor games and sports. It takes some time, but you'll need to find that sweet spot where these three considerations converge into a point of natural missional ministry.

Help! I'm in Stuck in _____ Model, but I Want to Take Middle Space Principles on Board!

I feel your pain here. I really do. What do you do when you work for a church in ministry that is firmly planted in another model, but you see the validity of Middle Space? At this point, we may need to go back to the drawing board. Let's revisit the principles again. Middle Space isn't really about space at all. It's about meeting with young people naturally and organically in a neutral ground. That neutral ground might not be a physical location at all. In other words, it may be possible for you to make small, but consistent, tweaks to your youth ministry over time, transitioning away from event-based ministry to something aimed more at long-term relationships, ethical evangelism, and faithful discipleship.

Even if you're working within a more or less Attractional ministry, can you have some conversations with both your leadership/supervisors as well as your volunteer team that could subtly but strategically shift the nature of the youth work you do? Can you make yourself more accessible relationally, not only to your existing, churchgoing young people, but to their friends, or to the young people in your own neighbourhood (taking into account the need for safeguarding and best practices)? Could you factor a day into your workweek where time is not spent in meetings or writing talks/preparing sessions, but instead in being intentional about building relationships outside the church walls? This may mean some important conversations with your supervisor about how your time is spent, but if you can make a case for it from a perspective of the long-term impact of the youth ministry, you may be surprised at how positively they respond.

Reflection Section

What are you most excited about when thinking of starting a Middle Space project?

What are you most intimidated by when thinking of starting a Middle Space project?

What are some key ideas you could take on board in your current setting?

What conversations do you need to have (with supervisors, key players, networks) to make it happen?

11

Middle Space in Practice

In this chapter, we're going to abandon the theory of Middle Space and, instead, look at a wide variety of places where Middle Space approaches to ministry are being utilized. These ministries vary greatly in their context. There are urban/city-centre churches, suburban churches, small-town arts centres, and intensely rural churches. They also vary greatly in what they offer. There are youth clubs, churches, skate parks, and ministries aimed at schools. There are even Middle Space ministries that don't meet young people at all, at least not in any literal sense! However, each of them is decidedly Middle Space in the way they are meeting with young people in a shared space – real or virtual. Because I've been working primarily in the United Kingdom for the past thirteen years, most of the examples reflect my observations there. However, there are certainly Middle Space ministries in the United States and elsewhere.

All Saints Church, Danehill, East Sussex, England
Rural youth club without a dedicated space

One church that is tackling the challenge of not having a dedicated space for youth ministry is All Saints Church in the tiny East Sussex village of Danehill. All Saints have the challenge that many rural Anglican churches have. That is, their beautiful, architectural churches don't have very flexible places for work with children and young people. Add to this the cultural barrier for those who don't normally attend church, and it's a real challenge for those who want to engage with young people in their area.

The youth ministry team at Danehill have approached the problem in a very pragmatic way – by hiring the local village hall. For readers not acquainted with English life, most parishes (urban or rural) will have a parish hall of some sort. These buildings are usually owned by the local council (or in Danehill's case, owned by a local trust) and intended specifically for local, public use. This can include anything from a toddler group to dance classes to private parties, and there is normally a small fee for using the building. All Saints rent their local hall weekly, hosting two open youth club sessions back-to-back on the same night of the week. Even though they don't have the benefit of owning their own building with exclusive use of the space, they've found a simple, yet creative way to make it work.

And it does indeed work, for a number of reasons. The first is that they know exactly what their goals are. They work primarily with unchurched young people, and they get several dozen young people through the doors of the hall each week – first in a session for younger teens, with the later session being dedicated to older teens. The groups are not explicitly religious, meaning these are not Bible study sessions or youth worship events, but the team also doesn't mind talking openly about the love of Jesus to whoever wants to listen. Not only do they get a lot of teens along to their weekly sessions, but they also manage to bring fifty to sixty kids along to an annual Christian camp. In fact, they are one of the largest groups at the camp each year, which is incredible considering the event is attended by groups from much larger churches and coming from much larger cities. They are able to achieve this by doing a very effective job of promoting the camp at their open youth clubs.

The second reason their open youth clubs work so well in the rented space is the way they've adapted their programming to fit their setting. Unlike our loose and unstructured approach to open youth clubs in Rudgwick (mentioned in chapter 7), the staff at Danehill have to be much more mindful of how they use both their space and their time. The main room in the hall is set up for sports and games. Table games like table tennis and foosball are set up in one half of the room. The other half is apportioned for sports using soft foam balls appropriate to the indoor setting. A floor-to-ceiling net separates the two halves of the room to keep stray balls from pummelling an unsuspecting attendee in the face. A small side room is set up with beads, string, paper, and a host of other craft supplies so those youngsters who want to express their creative side can try their hand at an artistic project. An adjacent room simply features sofas and hangout space. Unlike some clubs that may choose to keep their snack shop open for the entirety of the session, All Saints limit theirs to a short window of 15 or 20 minutes. All of this works in a neatly regimented form of chaos. The point is, they've adapted what space and time they have available to them, and they've made it work for their purposes.

The third thing they have going for them at All Saints is a really incredible team of people. Amazingly, the small rural church is able to employ a full-time youth worker, who also offers support to other small churches in the area who do not have a salaried youth pastor. However, they also have a strong base of volunteers. The husband and wife team of Steve and Meg have been serving the young people at Danehill for many years, and it was these volunteers who initiated the youth programme in its current form. Another thing that was really impressive is that the vicar (English for lead pastor) and his wife were also regular helpers at the youth clubs. When I visited, it was so refreshing to see a senior pastor serving on a team that he himself was not leading. Of particular note was his role in greeting parents at the door as they either dropped off or picked up their children. Imagine what kind of impact a pastor can have on local people who wouldn't ordinarily set foot in a church, just by showing up to do a menial task, or to say hello to people she or he wouldn't normally come into contact with!

Enrich, Bath, England
Urban youth club without a dedicated space

Another church-run youth ministry working largely with unchurched teens is Enrich in Bath. I first met Clive, a youth worker at Enrich (a ministry of All Saints Weston), a few years ago when I was doing some research into Middle Space approaches to youth work in the UK. I was trying to find out if there were other youth ministries taking a similar approach to what we were doing in Rudgwick. Although the work is in a much more urban setting, they have a similar approach to Middle Space youth work to both Rudgwick (my own context) and Danehill (above). Clive and his team run multiple sessions per week out of the Hub Centre in Weston (the far western edge of the city of Bath). What I find interesting about Clive's story is that he started out at his church in a more traditional youth ministry role. However, the longer he worked in the city and with churched youth, the more his heart ached to be reaching out to non-Christian teens. After praying about this for a considerable amount of time, and wondering if he'd have to leave his post, he sensed the Lord leading him to transition to outreach-oriented youth work in the same setting. With the approval of his supervisor, he was able to change the direction of his own youth work. At the same time, the church hired another youth pastor to continue the discipleship work with the existing church teens. This showed an amazing sense of partnership in the church leadership to do both discipleship based youth ministry and outreach-oriented youth work, although in this case, they functioned as two separate arms of the youth work.

The sessions at the Hub are based around social gatherings, fun and games, and sports. They have access to an outdoor, all-weather soccer/basketball combination court. Like Danehill (and unlike Rudgwick) they too do not have exclusive access to the building they use, so they have to set up and tear down before and after each session. What is strikingly different about this ministry is that, being in an urban area, they get a noticeably different crowd of young people that are more mobile (with more access to public transport) and more multicultural. Because of their urban neighbourhood location, they also get foot traffic from young people who are passing by and notice that something exciting is happening at the Hub.

One of the most innovative integrations of faith and open access youth work I've ever come across was here at Enrich, and it was truly Middle Space in every sense of the term. After the normal open session, Clive hosts a short, half-hour add-on session simply called "Check it Out". He makes it clear that it's additional to the normal hangout session, but that it's free and anyone is welcome. During the main session, I overheard him asking several teens, "Hey, are you staying for Check it Out?" Those who elected to stay were invited inside to one of the smaller breakout rooms, where there was a TV screen with an incredibly wide range of phrases on it, describing various perceptions or feelings about God. Some of the phrases included were:

- God? What a load of rubbish!
- I love God and I want to know him more.
- I'm not really sure what I think.
- I wish I could believe in God, but I don't.
- I wish I didn't believe in God, but I do.
- It's just not a priority in my life.

There were probably a dozen more phrases. Young people and adult helpers alike were asked to identify which of the statements on the screen best reflected their own views or thoughts on God. Because Clive had been working with them for such a long time, there was enough trust and mutual respect in the room to attempt such an in-depth – not to mention vulnerable – conversation. To my amazement, most of the young people very openly and honestly answered the question, with only one or two opting out of responding. Not surprisingly, answers were all over the spectrum, from those who affirmed faith in some way to those who had no affinity for it whatsoever. After everyone had a turn to answer, some discussion continued with young people being encouraged to be open to the possibility of God and his love for them. I found this a really great way to engage with young people around issues of faith, in an ethical, responsible, and friendly manner. It was open, honest, invitational, and non-coercive.

Legacy XS, South Benfleet, Essex, England
Suburban skate park ministry

Legacy XS is a youth centre whose primary function is as an indoor skate park. Having opened in 2005, the skate park is the primary youth ministry venue for St George's Church. The centre is open five days a week for open sessions, closing only on Fridays and Sundays (but available for private hire on those days). Most sessions involve a small fee to enter, normally £2 per session. Because they exist primarily as an indoor skate park, on sunny days they tend to have very low attendance, whereas on days when the weather is not so nice, particularly in the winter, they might see forty young people in a single session. Their attendance database of active members numbers well over 900 young people (meaning they have a completed consent form and have attended at least one session that year), although on a sunny day they may have fewer than ten young people. The local setting of Legacy XS is suburban – in the small town of South Benfleet in Essex, about an hour east of London. There are sports fields nearby, and also an outdoor football/basketball court, so it is clearly an area where young people naturally congregate. The centre is located in the heart of the community and is easy to get to. It's a prime location for a Middle Space youth ministry.

Of particular interest are two events which bring Middle Space youth work to the forefront: Scooter Church and Skate Church. These events are held on Tuesday afternoons and evenings, respectively. Whereas most of the open sessions at Legacy require a fee to take part, Scooter Church and Skate Church are free to attend, with one small caveat. Attendees are given free access to the ramps for a limited period of time, after which there is a short discussion featuring Christian content. For instance, past discussions have been centred on the Ten Commandments.

Because the youth centre is fully given to being a skate park, this leaves very little room (literally or figuratively) for much else other than skate park activities. Although there is an intense amount of dedication to this particular model – admirably so – it does make one wonder what will happen if or when the local culture changes and skate parks are no longer in demand for youth provisions. This question will have to be in the background somewhere as the team continue to reach out to youth in the area. It also touches on the philosophical issue of the problem of buildings; though buildings help enable ministry, they can also limit what kinds of ministry can take place, a point which is also true for church buildings!

Legacy is a very innovative and appropriate Middle Space youth ministry in a number of ways. In addition to the skate park facility, there is a small art centre upstairs in a separate room. This space is also hired out by a local dance school, bringing in income for the centre, but also serving to "cross-pollinate", or serve various needs in the community and encourage working together across different agencies.

As we seek to understand what we do in youth ministry and why we do it, lead youth worker Matt Rose articulated what he saw as the four steps of the transformative journey in young people, drawn in large part from his own testimony of coming to Christ: Hear – Listen – Pay Attention – Experience. *Hear.* Young people attend a group or session as passive participants. At this point, they are only "hearing" what is being said. *Listen.* As elements of the faith, or the lifestyle of other participants start to stick, young people move from simply hearing to listening. *Pay attention.* Further immersion in the group or culture drives them to begin paying attention to what is said, to how they feel as they are cared for and shown grace. *Experience.* The ultimate goal is that they experience God's love and grace for themselves, and see themselves as members of the faith community.

Another interesting observation was the role of religious art and displays. Legacy has the appearance of a non-religious environment. It is not a "church" per se, nor a sacred space in the strict sense. Yet, along the walls in the lounge are religious symbols and displays, as well as posters and information regarding skate culture. In the skate park itself hangs a large wicker figure representing Jesus on the cross, which was given to them by a Catholic church that no longer had use of it. The subtle yet powerful role of sacred art in a shared space is important in helping to create an atmosphere where faith is encouraged in non-threatening ways.

It's worth here including a final note about Legacy's journey of funding. When the church committed to opening a full-time skate park to be utilized in youth ministry, funding for the project started rolling in. Clearly God was involved in the timing and fundraising, because within a matter of months, the new-build project was fully funded! Much of this funding came via grants and funds available through local and regional councils, who were keen to back the project. This should be an encouragement to anyone who is considering taking on a new project and worried about funding.

The Grand, Clitheroe, Lancashire, northern England Suburban arts centre

The Grand is a renovated movie theatre in the heart of Clitheroe. Its stated purpose is, "Transforming lives and building community through the two arms of Faith, and the Arts". I love how clearly defined and distinct their statement of purpose is. The history of the Grand goes back to 1999 and has roots in a music and creative arts-based youth ministry in Bristol (south-west England). The building that the Grand now occupies used to be a cinema. It closed in 1999 and the Lancaster family purchased it in 2002.

The Grand runs a variety of events and activities that can be broken down into five categories:

- Events: these are generally music events or otherwise related to the arts and include things like music concerts, comedy, spoken word, theatre, and family events. Most of these will be ticketed events. Often, there is not a specific faith component, so they are aimed at the second part of the stated purpose, "building community through... the Arts". They have various "audiences" for different events (a jazz audience, a folk audience, a theatre audience, etc.). However, they also have very loyal patrons who will book for almost every event they run, and hence become part of the Grand community.
- Creative classes: these classes run the gamut from ballroom dancing to creative toddler groups to "Be My Band", an initiative where young people can learn a musical instrument and take part in kids' jam

sessions. There are also theatre and dance classes for children and young people.

- Creative learning: The Grand has an extensive creative learning project with local schools. They target children who might be less traditionally academic but have strengths in creative areas and work with them in conjunction with their schools. They also get involved in school assemblies and some mentoring through a gap year project called Pais, a discipleship programme for university-aged students and young adults.
- Community outreach: The Grand hosts a regional worship event once per month, and also owns and runs the town skate park. In fact, the Grand employs a youth worker part-time to run events and do outreach at the skate park (this youth worker also works as a youth pastor part-time in a local church, thus taking him to full-time capacity).
- Studio/venue: Lastly, the company owns and operates a recording studio. The studio is utilized in some of the educational projects with children, but can also be hired for local/regional recording projects and thus serves as a source of income for the project. Hired use of the studio results in an average of 20 hours a week usage. The venue itself can also be hired out for events.

Although not strictly a youth ministry, I include the Grand here as an example of a true Middle Space approach to ministry and outreach. Most of the staff are committed Christians, but volunteer staff at the Grand are comprised of both Christians and non-believers, showing that they take a Middle Space approach even amongst their teams. Second, there is a Middle Space approach to outreach. The Grand is not a church (nor is it connected to one specific congregation or church body), so their outreach ministry is taking place in a sort of neutral territory. Third, the work of the Grand involves faith in both explicit and indirect ways: explicitly through discipleship and worship events; indirectly through the lives and influence of the leadership, as well as through the ethos of the project itself.

Lastly, it's worth pointing out some convergence with Middle Space as shared by the leadership at the Grand. When asked about the development of the project, CEO/founder Steven Lancaster claimed that the ministry and work of the Grand had ended up where it is now because it had "evolved organically". This is a key theological foundation of Middle Space ministry, as discussed in chapter 5. True Middle Space work must be allowed to be missional/incarnational, and to be so it has to evolve naturally and organically based on the needs of the local context and the gifts of the leadership.

Another observation results from a question asked by manager Dave Thornber, who posed, "How do you go beyond 'middle ground' to doing discipleship?" This question hits at the heart of the ambiguous fusion between discipleship and evangelism. Dave didn't necessarily have the answer, but he was asking the right question. Perhaps the answer is found in the story of one of the Grand's volunteers. The Grand employs a number of people and also has a large team of volunteers. One such volunteer did not come from a faith background. Over time, she came to pick up something of the ethos and approach to community building and began also attending the worship gatherings. This woman was often seen lifting her arms slightly during the worship times. At one point she quipped to Dave, "I think the Grand has saved me." She has implicitly picked up on the essence of the purpose of the Grand: transforming lives and building community through faith and the arts. How then does one go about helping her on her discipleship journey? It might be messy and ambiguous, but her life is evidence that discipleship is, in fact, happening at the Grand.

Hot Chocolate Trust, Dundee, Scotland (based at Steeple Church)
Urban/city-centre youth work within an existing church building

One of the more interesting and unusual approaches to Middle Space youth work I've come across is a project in the city centre of Dundee, Scotland called Hot Chocolate Trust (HCT). HCT operates out of Steeple Church, a Church of Scotland congregation. They work largely with young people in "alternative culture". The roots of the organization go back to 2001, when the church hired a part-time youth worker. Unsure of how or where to start doing youth work, they noticed a large crowd of young people who gathered (or loitered) outside the church on a grassy spot. So they decided to try to get to know *those* young people – to get to know their stories. They began by offering cups of hot chocolate. Initially, they were not even trying to start a project. Their only agenda was just getting to know young people. I can't think of a more organic and natural way to start doing youth work. Generally speaking, a church decides they want to do youth ministry and then they start planning events to "draw young people in". Steeple Church did something entirely more effective: "Hey, there's some young people right on our front lawn. What if we tried to get to know them?" It's such a simple approach, but at the same time quite revolutionary!

As that work grew, they began to ask the young people, "If you had some space indoors, what would you want to do with it?" They found that a lot of the young people were in bands. Some of them were playing thrash metal and other genres that would not typically be welcomed into a church setting. So the church began giving them space to practise their material and to perform. Over time, HCT developed into what it is today by asking three simple questions, directed at young people:

- Who are you and what are your stories?
- What are you interested in?
- How can we support you in that?

The Trust now works with around 350–400 young people per year. Many of them are facing a variety of difficult issues. Around 86 per cent have some type of experience with the criminal justice system, either because they themselves have been in trouble with the law, or because a family member is in prison. Roughly 62 per cent are LGBTQ. However, Hot Chocolate Trust does not start with the negative or traumatic. Instead, they try to focus on the positive and what they can offer, focusing on the young people's strengths, talents, and their larger stories. The approach does not consist of simply vague praise, but specific things. For instance, "You are incredible on the guitar – can you show me how you do that?"

HCT became an independent charity in 2004 due to its growth and need for structure. Yet, it's housed within the church building. They have fifteen paid staff (a mixture of part-time and full-time), twenty volunteers per week, and around sixty to seventy throughout the year. Many of these are former young people. They are very intentional in how they transition young people into adult helpers, careful to not simply prolong their state of adolescence or create a long-term dependency on the youth work.

Although housed in the church building, HCT has a number of dedicated spaces in the church that are specific to the cause: sports room, art room, music room, sports hall, kitchen, chill room, cocoon room, etc. Assistant director Charis Robertson explains: "It's always felt like we were doing detached work from inside." This illustrates the principle that, more than being a physical location, Middle Space is a philosophical model of youth work. It also demonstrates how a Middle Space approach can be utilized inside existing church spaces and structures.

A further aspect of the Middle Space capacity at Hot Chocolate Trust is demonstrated by their approach to shared power in their relationships with young people. Rather than simply providing a service *for* young people or directed *at* them, they ask young people, "What do you want to do?" Robertson makes it clear that they are not a service at all, but rather growing a community with them. Having said that, HCT provides a number of services that the young people themselves are engaged in. These services align with their eight target outcomes, which we'll discuss below.

Regarding the interplay between the Christian faith and their open approach to relational youth work, Robertson explains, "They don't come to us because they are exploring Christianity, but because they have found a safe space. The young people know it's a Christian organization." In fact, the organization has a list of eight target outcomes for young people, one of which is spirituality.

The eight outcomes are as follows:

- that young people grow in self-worth
- that young people grow in self-knowledge
- that young people improve their social skills
- that young people increase in understanding that they can positively impact their lives and communities
- that young people act to positively impact their lives and communities
- that young people improve their ability to plan ahead and stick to goals
- that young people increase in their awareness and understanding of their spirituality
- that young people move into positive destinations: employment, education, and/or training.

It is worth noting that outcome 7, regarding spirituality, is where the connection to the church and Christian youth work is most visible. In fact, Hot Chocolate Trust employs one full-time youth worker dedicated to this task.

Furthermore, Hot Chocolate Trust focuses on the following core values:

- holistic development which realizes physical, mental, emotional, and spiritual potential
- a place that is open, responsive, safe, accepting, and grows community
- relationships based on respect and trust, which are organic and reciprocal
- plans and activities owned by young people, that adapt with culture and realize change for all involved
- an organization that embodies a culture of reflective learning.

Motus Dance Academy, Bath, England
Targeted youth work, focused on the arts; needs-based youth work

Chris Porter leads a creative approach to Middle Space youth work in the form of the Motus Dance Academy. The name comes from the Latin word for dance or performance. Chris takes his love of, and skills in, dance and helps to run a dance school for young people, along with another youth worker. The two of them run sessions for 11 to 18-year-olds and have a core group of fifteen with a few more who take part less regularly. The group incorporates informal education in performing arts, as well as relationship-building. This facilitates many chats around faith, which are allowed to come up in a very natural and unforced way, simply by being together and by sometimes utilizing church spaces. One of the buildings they use for rehearsals is a Methodist church, and sometimes simple questions arise like, "Why is there a cross there?" Chris explains, "Just by being ourselves, conversations [about faith] happen."

When asked what drives his approach with the dance school, Chris articulated that it's "Kingdom not Empire". When asked to unpack this a bit more, he told me that Christian youth work should be about building up the kingdom of God, not our own empires. We talked about how difficult it is to measure good youth work. So much of what happens in Christian youth work cannot be counted easily in numbers alone. Chris and the team have a truly Middle Space approach that is flexible, fluid, and has evolved naturally and organically (and continues to do so). Additionally, in his work with Bath Youth for Christ, Chris does work in local schools, as well as hosting a daily breakfast club, providing a free, simple breakfast for children and young people who might otherwise go to school without having had breakfast.

Andy Gray, Somerset, England
Gaming in youth work (role-playing games and board games)

Gray has been working with children and young people for over twenty-five years, often in churches, but also spent nine years working for Scripture Union, and has spent time working in schools and with youth congregations. For nearly ten years, Andy has been an illustrator for a UK publishing house, and served as an ordained "pioneer minister" in the Church of England, a specially trained position with a focus on creating churches where church doesn't exist. Even this aspect of his work has largely focused on children and young people.

For that same twenty-five years, Gray has been a hardcore gamer. He recalls, "When I first started working with young people they introduced me to war-gaming (Necromunda) and I introduced them to RPG [role-playing games] – dice, not video games, and used RPG to help them explore faith in action." Gray found gaming to be a unique way to interact with young people, particularly those with special needs: Asperger syndrome, autism, dyslexia, dyspraxia, and other neuro-atypical conditions. He made this discovery while playing board games with his own son and his three friends, each of whom had some sort of special need or neuro-atypical condition. "Gaming helped all of them and they were basically my youth group." He found that as the young people relaxed around the game, he was able to talk about faith in a natural and non-coercive way. He's also quick to point out that although one might use the analogy of the board game to talk about faith, it's far more interesting to use the experience which each game brings to explore spirituality. In essence, the game board itself becomes the Middle Space, around which life is shared and faith is explored.

Eventually, Gray's work with his son and friends led to establishing a board game community, which also largely helped to serve the local autistic community. Over time, 30–50 per cent of the people who took part were from families where some aspect of Asperger's, ADHD, or autism was present. The majority of the members were not a part of other activities or communities like sports, drama, or music. Although all ages were represented, fully half of those involved were children and young people. This work also led to the creation of an online gaming network that other ministers and youth workers around the UK could utilize for gaming ministry and building community. Thus, another area of Middle Space was created in the form of the use of digital space or virtual space.

Gray's work in gaming consists of four simple ways that gaming can be used effectively in youth ministry:

- It allows us to connect with people we might not normally connect with, or with people who may not engage with other aspects of our youth work.
- It helps us to discover "the geeks and the freaks" who aren't necessarily sporty, or who don't have a wealth of friendships. Thus, gaming ministry helps aim at the heart of the gospel by connecting people to friendships and enabling them to live out the second commandment to love one's neighbour.
- It allows people to engage educationally with links to schools through the mental, cognitive, and sociological benefits of gaming, particularly for young people with special needs.
- It creates a Middle Space in which to interact and explore themes of faith and spirituality, through the shared environment of the gaming board.

Somewhat unsurprisingly, Gray has also been diagnosed with Asperger's, which is perhaps why he is so effective at this type of ministry. He explains that, often, "We don't get hidden social cues. I trained myself in body language when I was a teenager, in order to cope. We also don't get when things change (unless we are in charge and there are rules). So gaming is awesome. We know when it's our turn to talk. The game has order. We get to use our logical or lateral thinking brains. We can obsess over rule books."

Gray's work with gaming raises a whole host of possibilities around how we define Middle Space. I'm currently writing amidst the coronavirus pandemic (which will hopefully have subsided by the time you are reading this). Covid-19 is forcing many of us to rethink how we do ministry, not the least consideration of which is how to engage with people via virtual spaces. Gray offers a final sobering thought: "The hardest part of being autistic means a lack of friendship. So if you want to help a very hidden group in society and tell them of the friend who will never leave or forget them, start a games group."

St Alban's Church Frant with Holy Trinity Church Eridge, Frant (and Eridge), East Sussex, England
Festival Church: rural, outdoor youth and children's ministry

To understand what Festival Church is all about, we first need to backtrack to the Scandinavian concept of "forest school". Forest school is an outdoor learning process that has really taken off in many European countries in recent years. Many primary schools in the UK, for instance, spend time outdoors learning in nearby woodland, if they have access to it. There is quite a lot of educational theory behind it, as children learn in a variety of activities like lighting fires, building outdoor dens/forts, climbing trees, and practising woodland arts and crafts like making bows and arrows, swords, and bird feeders. Motor skills are developed through work with tools, and the children benefit from the close contact with nature. The fresh air doesn't hurt either! Children and adults who participate develop in confidence, imagination, teamwork, self-esteem, and social skills like cooperation, compromise, and conflict resolution.

Festival Church was developed when youth and children's worker Ed Pascoe caught a vision for utilizing a similar approach in the local church. Ed's journey began when, as part of his own professional development, he trained to be a certified Forest School Instructor. He was seeing more and more schools in the area providing outdoor learning experiences, but had not seen anything like it in the Church. He wondered what it would look like to develop an outdoor approach to ministry, evangelism, and discipleship. The church in Frant underwent a leadership change in 2019. During one of the early staff meetings, Revd Brendan Martin shared his vision for using outdoor services: worshipping the God of creation *in creation*! Pascoe, as youth and children's worker, was overjoyed, as it seemed that the new pastor's vision of outdoor worship neatly aligned with his passion and vision for outdoor children's ministry.

However, Pascoe's insights are much deeper than a mere coincidence. Frant is a decidedly rural location with legitimate contextualized needs of ministry. He observes, "The model that city churches use is often replicated by smaller rural churches, and in my opinion, usually doesn't work. We wanted to do something new, out of the box and using the resources that our church had here." This is a clear illustration of the Middle Space concept of contextualization, with nods to a natural and organic evolution of ministry practices.

They've also gotten lots of mileage out of using the space and facilities that they already had. For instance, next to the church's rectory there is a paddock and a small area of woodland. After many hours of cutting, chopping, and hacking to prepare the space, they began hosting outdoor Sunday school groups. They have erected a large, open marquee, where larger meetings meet with live music, talks, discussion groups, and prayers. There are mini fire pits that accommodate up to six people (even with social distancing measures during Covid). In the adjacent woodland are more fire pits, log seating, and parachute-style canopies over each. The children engage in discussion groups around a warm campfire, complete with Bible stories, discussion about Jesus, and of course the expected woodland fare: outdoor games, tree climbing, woodland crafts, etc. Much of the discussion in the groups is themed around the God of creation. In fact, the slogan of Festival Church is encapsulated in the three Cs: Creation, Community, and Creator.

The sessions began in September of 2020, with thirteen children taking part in the first meeting. It quickly grew to thirty, split into two smaller groups of fifteen each. There is now a waiting list to take part, so that they can keep the groups safe and maintain a healthy ratio of adult leaders to children. Pascoe exclaims, "I've been here just over four years and I've never had that number of kids turning up on a Sunday for church." When I asked him how many of the children taking part in Festival Church were from non-churchgoing families, he informed me that nearly all of them were. Talk about success in bridge-building with people who wouldn't normally attend church! They've since seen five new local families join the church, each of them a family with multiple children. Most of these would be described as those who would normally be hesitant to step into a church building but love coming to an outdoor service.

Brookside Community Church, Indianapolis, Indiana, USA
Urban/inner-city, needs-based

Brookside Community Church (BCC) is a relatively young church plant in the Near Eastside neighbourhood in Indianapolis. It was originally started as a satellite congregation of a suburban megachurch, but over time it has become independent, while coexisting as a sister church. The symbiosis was achieved largely as the result of leadership in both locations realizing the unique contextual needs in each location were very different. Amazingly, while allowing Brookside autonomy, Northview

Church still assists it with resources: financial help, people resources, and access to staff and training.

Of particular interest to Middle Space youth work is BCC's initiative simply called "Play". Begun in 2016, "Play exists to provide structured play opportunities that help children and youth grow emotionally, spiritually, physically, and academically." Because the church resides in a neighbourhood of intense inter-generational poverty, high crime, and violence, they found that the children and young people of the area they met were carrying various kinds of trauma. So Play began largely as a way to help children *be* children and to help them beat the odds of their neighbourhood – a neighbourhood where 65–70 per cent of families live below the national poverty level, where 10 per cent of residents have been victims of a violent crime, and where 4 per cent of children under eighteen have been through the juvenile justice system.

Initially, Play existed for children, but BCC's work with youth evolved out of it. Older siblings started showing up at their doors saying, "You do all this stuff for my little brother, what are you gonna do for me?" So, true to Middle Space principles, Play added youth programming to its already impressive work, known as Brookside Community Play Education & Employment Academy. Although Play is fully integrated into the ministry of Brookside Community Church, their work with teenagers focuses on "developing passion, purpose, and hope through education and employability".[37]

The Academy features four days of weekly programming, as well as additional summer programming and day camps. During the school term, each day features a different emphasis. Mondays are spent on Leadership Development through group exercises, guest speakers, and unique opportunities for growth and personal transformation. Tuesdays see a focus on tutoring and academic planning through high school and preparation for college or university. Teens are challenged to imagine their future and assisted in developing a plan to achieve it. Wednesdays focus on employment opportunities. Young people can gain experience in hands-on employment opportunities, and earn either a paycheque (if old enough) or educational awards and invaluable experience for the future. Thursdays are spent helping young people develop "Sparks", discovering their passions and personal interests. A fifth element of the Academy is mentoring. Teenagers are connected with long-term mentors who support their social, emotional, and spiritual development.

Does Play work? In 2018 alone, sixty-four children and young people participated in after-school programmes. One hundred and seventy-five participated in summer programming and thirty-eight participated in play camps. A total of 750 hours of play-based programming was offered throughout the year. As for the results, 84 per cent of participants experience some form of improvement to their social and emotional well-being. 100 per cent of participants reported making a new friend through Play, and 100 per cent also reported they were able to solve a problem utilizing a skill learned at Play.[38]

In regards to the creative use of space, Brookside have created classroom space within the church building that is solely used for Play. The majority of the children and young people who take part in Play are not church members. Many of them would not be found in a church at all, so it was important that Play had a welcoming environment for the exclusive use of those taking part. Additionally, all programmes are offered free of charge, as opposed to many other after-school programmes in the area that charge a fee for their services.

I find two things about Brookside Community Church fascinating. First, Play (and other initiatives we haven't mentioned, such as their work in Housing and Re-Entry) was birthed out of a local church that simply wanted to make a difference in their community. Second, their approach to Middle Space was achieved not through the creative use of non-church space – most of their programming (sans field trips and outdoor activities) takes place within the church building – but rather through finding needs within their community and then committing to journeying with people towards Jesus. This needs-based approach has led them to recreate and reimagine spaces within the church to make their participants feel more at home, but it's all happened within the existing church building. We'll say more below about other needs-based approaches to Middle Space.

Other Ways of Achieving Middle Space

As we conclude our section on Middle Space practices and examples on the ground, it's worth thinking through a number of categories in which Middle Space exists. Above, we've examined Middle Space in rural, suburban, and urban contexts. We've considered youth ministries that have dedicated space that is separate from a church building, dedicated space within a church building, and those who don't have a building to themselves but use multi-use spaces. We've seen examples of ministries that use outdoor spaces and even virtual spaces in which to do youth work. Let's look at a few trends that overlap with Middle Space, while not reflecting on a particular location.

A large branch of Christian youth work in the United Kingdom is schools work. This is when a youth worker is employed by a church or charity – or in some cases, by the school itself – to do youth work within the school setting. Many church-based youth workers (including myself) engage in some level of schools work on a semi-regular basis, whereas others work primarily within the school setting full-time. The question for our purposes here is, "In what ways can schools work be considered Middle Space?" Although I tend to see schools work as a distinct model in its own right, it's hard to ignore the parallels with Middle Space. It may be tempting to see the school as "their space" and therefore not a meeting in the middle. However, I think it's difficult to argue that schools are spaces which are owned by the young people, in no small part because they are required to be there. The fact that young people are required by law to attend school (up to a certain age) means that the school setting cannot in any definitive way be considered *their* space.

Dan Randall leads a large schools work ministry in four different high schools in Burnley in northern England. He also leads the youth work at LifeChurch and helps lead the Pais movement (a gap-year ministry for young adults). Dan sees a lot of overlap between his three areas. Pais missionaries serve in the schools work setting; young people who have made connections through the schools work sometimes end up in the youth group of LifeChurch. As an interesting and compelling side note, Dan grew up in Barrow-in-Furness, where he himself went to an open-access youth club. As a seventeen-year-old, he got involved in helping to lead activities there.

Their schools work runs lunch clubs, which function similarly to a Christian Union or faith club at school. Across those four different clubs, their work sees around 200 kids per week. Many of these young people do not come from church/faith backgrounds, yet a number of them have journeyed to involvement at Friday night youth group at LifeChurch or gotten involved elsewhere. Remarkably, they have even seen some conversions take place in the lunch clubs themselves! Again, this begs the observation that schools work can indeed function as Middle Space

– meeting young people on a middle ground that is neither theirs nor ours, and having conversations around faith in a non-coercive environment. It's also important to note that the work in Burnley began by simply approaching the head teachers with the question, "How can our youth work support your work here in the school?"

Another area that is seeing some development of the Middle Space ethos is that of service-based or needs-based youth ministry. Although we have highlighted aspects of this with Brookside Community Church in America, there are loads of further possibilities in a variety of contexts. UK-based charity TLG (Transforming Lives for Good) also works primarily in schools, but with targeted, needs-based approaches. They work primarily with children who are struggling in school for a number of reasons: poor behaviour, poverty, lack of access to food and nutrition, and a whole host of other areas. TLG's strengths lie in the way it partners local churches with local schools, providing training for people who want to serve children in their areas, helping them to succeed and achieve academic success. Although there may be similar ministries in the United States, I am not aware of them working in any widespread capacity.

This begs a larger question: what other ways can service-based and needs-based youth work become a targeted way of doing Middle Space? How can we explore things like sports ministry that works with a broad spectrum of young people from varying degrees of faith background? What about a church or youth ministry that offers a life skills course to older teens preparing for university or a life of independence? Many young people would benefit from instruction on balancing a budget, basic cooking skills, shopping (how to feed and clothe yourself healthily on a limited budget), minor car maintenance and repairs, and a whole host of related issues. Attractional ministry is rarely focused on these kinds of services, as their top priorities tend to be figuring out how to get more people to one of their events.

Reflection Section

Which of these Middle Space stories resonates with you the most?

Which of these Middle Space stories surprises you the most?

How can you see the Lord working in your own life or in your ministry setting to bring about a similar innovation in your youth work?

12

Afterword

Now that we're coming to the end of our journey together, perhaps it's time to go right back to where we started. In the first part of this book, I said that I wanted to give you a tool for reflection, something to help the youth work community think about what we do and why we do it. Now, it's time to go and do it. For those of you just starting out, I give you permission to dream. Permission to try some things that may or may not work – permission to fail, *and* to learn from those failures and carry on in new and more productive ways. Remember our observation earlier: if you haven't tried something that's failed, you may not be risking enough.

For those of you who are already in the trenches, I simply want to leave you with lots of permissions. Permission to try again. To cast your nets to the other side at the bidding of Jesus. To spread your net farther and wider, or more narrowly and specifically as he leads. Permission to listen to the Holy Spirit, and discern the needs, as well as the prospects, of your local context. I release you to go and have difficult and/or interesting conversations with your supervisor. And finally, I charge you with the joyful task of having to ask for help, and to ask great people to join your team. Go now and prayerfully challenge the status quo in pursuing an apostolic model of ministry. Go and find your Middle Space – not ours, not theirs, just somewhere in the middle.

Endnotes

1 https://www.dictionary.com/browse/entertain.

2 Kenda Creasy Dean, *Almost Christian* (Oxford: Oxford University Press, 2010), p.160.

3 Richard Passmore, *Meet Them Where They're at* (Bletchley: Scripture Union, 2003); and Richard and Lorimer Passmore, *Here Be Dragons: Youth Work and Mission off the Map* (Birmingham: Frontier Youth Trust, 2013).

4 Sylvia Collins-Mayo, Bob Mayo, Sally Nash, with Christopher Cocksworth, *The Faith of Generation Y* (London: Church House Publishing, 2010), p.4.

5 UK-based parachurch ministry Tearfund's research in 2007 found that roughly 10 per cent of the population in the UK attend church "regularly". In this study, regular church attendance was defined by attending services at least once per month. Fringe church attendance was defined as going at least six times per year, and occasional church attendance meant at least once per year. J. Ashworth and I. Farthing, "Churchgoing in the UK: A Research Report from Tearfund on Church Attendance in the UK", *BBC News*, http://news.bbc.co.uk/1/shared/bsp/hi/pdfs/03_04_07_tearfundchurch.pdf (last viewed 14 March 2021).

6 Ashworth and Farthing, *Churchgoing in the UK* (Tearfund, 2007).

7 Peter Brierley, *Pulling out of the Nosedive* (London: Christian Research, 2006), p.12.

8 Collins-Mayo et al., *The Faith of Generation Y*, p.5.

9 A succinct definition of the term and how it has developed can be found in Christian Smith and Melinda Lundquist Denton, *Soul Searching: The Religious and Spiritual Lives of American Teenagers* (Oxford: Oxford University Press, 2005).

10 K. Creasy-Dean, *Almost Christian*, p.127, but see also chapter 4 on the importance of "Generative Faith."

11 Creasy-Dean, *Almost Christian*, p.17.

12 Youth for Christ, *Z-A of Faith & Spirituality* (Halesowen: Youth for Christ, 2020), p.36.

13 Alan Hirsh, *The Forgotten Ways*, second ed. (Grand Rapids, MI: Brazos Press, 2016), p.37.

14 This line is taken from the film *Field of Dreams* in which the main character is instructed by a dead baseball player to build a baseball field in his backyard and subsequently is visited by departed baseball legends. *Field of Dreams*, directed by Phil Alden Robinson, Universal, 1989.

15 Eugene Peterson, *Five Smooth Stones for Pastoral Work* (Grand Rapids, MI: Wm. B. Eerdmans, 1980), pp.212–13.

16 Mark Mittelberg and Lee Strobel, *Becoming a Contagious Christian: Youth Edition Student's Guide* (Grand Rapids, MI: Zondervan, 2001).

17 Here we are using the term in a generic sense, to refer to any youth work that takes place unattached to a church or other sponsored building or space. We are not referring to any one specific model of youth ministry. For more on Detached youth work, see Richard Passmore's *Meet Them Where They're at* and also Richard and Lorimer Passmore's *Here Be Dragons: Youth Work and Mission off the Map*.

18 "Symbiotic youth work" is the form of Detached youth work Richard and Lorimer Passmore advocate for in *Here Be Dragons*. The focus is on meeting young people in the spaces where they normally congregate – not to invite them into church, but instead, by building trusting relationships with them, to forge ahead and create altogether new forms of church.

19 Bonfire Night (or alternately Guy Fawkes Night or Fireworks Night) is a commemoration of the stifled plot to blow up the House of Lords in 1605. In such observances, local events are hosted with a bonfire, fireworks, and other forms of entertainment, in a somewhat patriotic celebration not too unlike the 4 July celebrations in the United States. The events are held on or around 5 November each year.

20 Mark Yaconelli, *Contemplative Youth Ministry* (London: SPCK, 2006), p.51.

21 The Fresh Expressions movement is an ecumenical movement in the United Kingdom, birthed out of the Church of England officially in 2004, though its roots are in the 1990s. It reflects a "growing number of re-imagined church communities" and "a recognition and provision for those seeking to work with changing culture and those not yet attending church". Fresh Expressions, "About", *Fresh Expressions*, https://freshexpressions.org.uk/about/ (last viewed 13 March 2021).

22 Richard Passmore has rightly criticized this form of bridge-building in *Here Be Dragons*.

23 It was very obvious in the early days that as a 35-year-old American man, we would have to create natural and appropriate ways to build relationships with teenagers in healthy and safe ways – particularly those outside the church family. We'll talk more about safeguarding and making Middle Space sustainable in chapters 8 and 9.

24 For more on the concept of "incarnational ministry" see Michael Frost and Alan Hirsch, *The Shaping of Things to Come* (Peabody, MA: Hendrickson, 2006), particularly chapter 3, "The Incarnational Approach".

25 Creasy-Dean, *Almost Christian*, p.183.

26 Creasy-Dean, *Almost Christian*, p.37.

27 Creasy-Dean, *Almost Christian*, p.93.

28 Yaconelli, *Contemplative Youth Ministry*, pp.168–69.

29 Mark Ashton and Phil Moon, *Christian Youth Work*, revised ed. (Chorley: 10Publishing, 2007), p.62.

30 Hugh Halter and Matt Smay give a helpful, if simplified, overview of this in *Tangible Kingdom* (San Francisco, CA: Jossey-Bass, 2008), pp.55–57.

31 K. Creasy-Dean, citing situated learning theory, describes the importance of "peripheral, legitimate participation"; *Almost Christian*, pp.144–46.

32 Sally Nash, Sylvia Collins-Mayo, and Bob Mayo, "Raising Christian Consciousness: Creating Place," *Journal of Youth and Theology*, Volume 6, Number 2 (November 2007), p.46.

33 Nash, Collins-Mayo, and Mayo, "Raising Christian Consciousness," p.43.

34 Collins-Mayo et al., *The Faith of Generation Y*, p.76.

35 Collins-Mayo et al., *The Faith of Generation Y*, pp.77–78.

36 Peter Lattman, "The Origins of Justice Stewart's 'I Know When I See It'," *Wall Street Journal*, https://www.wsj.com/articles/BL-LB-4558 (last viewed 14 March 2021).

37 Brookside Community Play Education & Employment Academy, https://www.brooksideplay.org/academy (last viewed 14 March 2021).

38 All stats taken from https://www.brooksideplay.org/ (last viewed 14 March 2021).

Bibliography

Mark Ashton and Phil Moon, *Christian Youth Work*, revised ed. (Chorley: 10Publishing, 2007).

Jacinta Ashworth and Ian Farthing, "Churchgoing in the UK: A Research Report from Tearfund on Church Attendance in the UK", *BBC News*, http://news.bbc.co.uk/1/shared/bsp/hi/pdfs/03_04_07_tearfundchurch.pdf (last viewed 14 March 2021).

Peter Brierley, *Pulling out of the Nosedive* (London: Christian Research, 2006).

Sylvia Collins-Mayo, Bob Mayo, Sally Nash, with Christopher Cocksworth, *The Faith of Generation Y* (London: Church House Publishing, 2010).

Kenda Creasy-Dean, *Almost Christian* (Oxford: Oxford University Press, 2010).

Fresh Expressions, "About", *Fresh Expressions*, https://freshexpressions.org.uk/about/ (last viewed 13 March 2021).

Michael Frost and Alan Hirsch, *The Shaping of Things to Come* (Peabody, MA: Hendrickson, 2006).

Hugh Halter and Matt Smay, *Tangible Kingdom* (San Francisco, CA: Jossey-Bass, 2008).

Alan Hirsh, *The Forgotten Ways,* second ed. (Grand Rapids, MI: Brazos Press, 2016).

Mark Mittelberg and Lee Strobel, *Becoming a Contagious Christian: Youth Edition Student's Guide* (Grand Rapids, MI: Zondervan, 2001).

Peter Lattman, "The Origins of Justice Stewart's 'I Know When I See It'," *Wall Street Journal*, https://www.wsj.com/articles/BL-LB-4558 (last viewed 14 March 2021).

Sally Nash, Sylvia Collins-Mayo, and Bob Mayo, "Raising Christian Consciousness: Creating Place," *Journal of Youth and Theology*, Volume 6, Number 2 (November 2007), pp.41–59.

Richard Passmore, *Meet Them Where They're at* (Bletchley: Scripture Union, 2003).

Richard Passmore and Lorimer Passmore, *Here Be Dragons: Youth Work and Mission off the Map* (Birmingham: Frontier Youth Trust, 2013).

Bibliography

Eugene Peterson, *Five Smooth Stones for Pastoral Work* (Grand Rapids, MI: Wm. B. Eerdmans, 1980).

Christian Smith and Melinda Lundquist Denton, *Soul Searching: The Religious and Spiritual Lives of American Teenagers* (Oxford: Oxford University Press, 2005).

Mark Yaconelli, *Contemplative Youth Ministry* (London: SPCK, 2006).

Youth for Christ, *Z-A of Faith & Spirituality* (Halesowen: Youth for Christ, 2020).